GUIDEBOOK

HAUNTED
AND
STRANGE
PLACES
IN
RHODE
ISLAND
AND SURROUNDS

By Charles
Harrington

Schiffer
Publishing Ltd

4880 Lower Valley Road • Atglen, PA 19310

Illustrations by
Kristen Regan

Dedication

I dedicate this to my mother, Mary Harrington, who thought a library card was a better entertainment system than a video game console.

Cover design by Matt Goodman
Type set in Futura & Minion
ISBN: 978-0-7643-5195-2

Printed in China

Published by Schiffer Publishing, Ltd.
4880 Lower Valley Road
Atglen, PA 19310
Phone: (610) 593-1777; Fax: (610) 593-2002
E-mail: Info@schifferbooks.com
Web: www.schifferbooks.com

For our complete selection of fine books on this and related subjects, please visit our website at www.schifferbooks.com. You may also write for a free catalog.

Schiffer Publishing's titles are available at special discounts for bulk purchases for sales promotions or premiums. Special editions, including personalized covers, corporate imprints, and excerpts, can be created in large quantities for special needs. For more information, contact the publisher.

We are always looking for people to write books on new and related subjects.
If you have an idea for a book, please contact us at proposals@schifferbooks.com.

Contents

Introduction

IT.

All capitals and lacking in detail. That was what Howard Phillips Lovecraft and his friend Clifford Martin Eddy set out to find in 1923. IT was rumored to be in Dark Swamp (actual name) in northwestern Rhode Island and was a local legend, according to Henry L. Beckwith Jr. in *Lovecraft's Providence and Adjacent Parts*. The trip that Lovecraft and his friend took that day may be the first recorded supernatural tour in New England. While there have been reports of trips to cemeteries to look for vampires or investigate ghosts for centuries, this was a leisure trip, which set it apart and may have raised a few questions about the mental state of the participants.

Today, seekers of the strange can ask about the less ominous-sounding "doat" of Prudence Island at Prudence Variety Store, which is a meeting point for people from all walks of life in that small community. The wood-framed shop offers comforting cups of coffee and iced drinks on warmer days along with friendly chats and recommendations for how to get around. While a name like Dark Swamp implies some visitors not making a return trip, the mortality rate for Prudence Island is exceptionally low—the mysterious demise of James Garland at his mansion, detailed in the tour, being an exception to the statistics. If a person is looking for a more frightening beast, a trip through the dark corridors of Fort Wetherill in Jamestown may lead to a chance encounter with the Black Dog that has been allegedly haunting the area since colonial times.

On their journey, Lovecraft and his partner in monster hunting likely knocked on doors and questioned passersby looking for information; today's seekers of the macabre can look for better, detailed routes and maps in this book, one of numerous printed about New England legends but one of the few where oddities of the supernatural reside next to tales of interest all along a walking, or biking, route that can be enjoyed at the reader's leisure. If a person gets lost or the weather turns foul, as long as they survive the detour or infamously unpredictable New England weather, they can pick up where they left off at a time of their choosing.

Lovecraft in his quest for IT of Dark Swamp no doubt knew the importance of food and drink along the way and that is also addressed here as some of the most historical eating and drinking establishments in Rhode Island are described. If you're going to stop off for a bite to eat, do it someplace unique and not at a fast-food restaurant that is a clone of thousands. The White Horse Tavern in Newport is the oldest establishment of its kind in the United States and is where the Newport tour starts. Geoff's, a superb sandwich shop on Benefit Street in Providence, is a welcome site for hungry masses daily and caps the end of the tour past Lovecraft's haunts in the capital city. The Narragansett Café in Jamestown has been catering to the culinary and musical tastes of its clientele for decades and has won numerous awards in the process.

Lovecraft left his mark on the genre of "weird" fiction, but he also likely influenced a few people to take off and look for the strange and the haunted. Put on a comfortable pair of shoes or boots and head out for a trip; to date no one taking any of these tours has died at the hands of a mysterious creature lurking around the corner, so you should be fine. Feel free to bring an expendable acquaintance along, for pushing into the path of danger, just in case.

The Providence of H. P. Lovecraft & His Fiction

Providence skyline. Once covered with the largest bridge in the world, the Providence River is again exposed for visitors to enjoy.

A house is an empty shell without the stories and history that make it a home. While Howard Phillips Lovecraft will always be better known for his macabre tales and demonic mythology, he also wrote, almost as supporting characters, about the cities and homes that the characters inhabited. "The Case of Charles Dexter Ward," "The Call of Cthulu," and "The Shunned House" were given a sense of realism because of the attention to architectural detail Lovecraft found interesting and included as backdrop to his stories.

Instead of creating a fictional house at the end of an unnamed avenue, Lovecraft described a house that was abandoned on College Hill. Charles Dexter Ward did not merely ride by a generic landscape on his way home from abroad, he went past houses with long histories going back to the 1700s. Characters didn't die on nameless streets, they expired on winding avenues close to where Lovecraft the author was born and raised.

The city of Providence has seen numerous changes since Lovecraft first put pen to paper nearly 100 years ago and changed the face of horror fiction forever. Over those years, rivers have been covered in the name of progress and then exposed in the name of tourism, monuments to the dead have been disassembled and moved and one man's remains have been relocated so many times over the centuries that his latest, final resting place refers to his "dust" not bones. Throughout these changes some things have remained the same, including many of the buildings that Lovecraft populated in his imagination with vampires, mad scientists, and heroes.

Visitors today can stroll along the streets, some of which are still brick lined, and get a sense of the stories, history, and design that influenced the man that many consider to be one of the best and most influential horror writers of the twentieth century.

The Walking Tour

1 & 2 Kennedy Plaza & Providence City Hall
1 Kennedy Plaza & 25 Dorrance Street

It's a New England tradition to give directions not by what occupies a spot today but by what store or restaurant was once there. *Lovecraft's Providence & Adjacent Parts* by Henry L. P. Beckwith Jr., if read today, would introduce readers to the tradition in a truly maddening fashion.

The guidebook was mapped out in the 1970s and much has changed since the first steps were taken along the two-and-a-half to three-hour walking tour. Overflowing parking lots are now memorials, alleys, and streets and have been demolished to expose a river that was covered up to build office space and then exposed again in the 1990s to become a focal tourist attraction that welcomes hundreds of thousands in the summer months. Parts of the original written tour are unrecognizable to anyone who was not raised in Providence during the years of change. While the core has remained, the edges have become blurred beyond recognition.

One spot that hasn't changed much but has seen the edges blurred is Kennedy Plaza, formerly Post Office Square and Providence City Hall. Built in 1878, City Hall has hosted the usual suspects of mayors and city councilors as well as President Teddy Roosevelt, who gave a speech from the front steps, which are seldom opened to the public, and John F. Kennedy, who addressed a crowd in the plaza, which was later named for him days before being elected president.

The baroque-styled building is the focal piece of the plaza, and access to the marbled floors and wood-trimmed walls and bannisters of the interior can be had through the north- and south-side doors on street level.

Visitors are welcome but should remember that despite the vintage feel of the halls and offices, it is the center of city business and intrusive behavior is discouraged—unless of course you happen to be the ghost that allegedly resides around the archives room on the fifth floor. The ghost was a topic of an investigation by the television show *Ghosthunters* (which features paranormal investigators based in Rhode Island), and it has been seen and heard by staff for years.

Stalled elevators, smells of cigar smoke, and the odd bumps and sounds are some of the evidence collected by the investigators. The episode lacked any solid evidence of a haunting, such as video of shrieking banshees crawling through walls, but the circumstantial sounds and experiences are enough to keep some people wondering.

The wood-trimmed City Council Chamber and gallery is one of the few of its kind remaining in the country today. Most cities have switched to cloth-covered seats and imitation wood-lined walls, if not cheap plaster and plastic accents. The chambers here are wooden seats and benches in the gallery for visitors interested in seeing city government at work and presumably more comfortable seats for the councilors. Except for the occasional plastic-covered wall outlet and the odd water cooler, the chamber appears to have changed little in the century-plus since it was built. A stroll in the chamber and a visit to the gallery is strongly recommended if open.

Whether you see or hear the ghost or not, a walk amongst the halls and archives is suggested as a reminder of when records were kept in tomes, not in digital formats, and city planners used ink and paper to map boundaries, not computers and programs. Providence City Hall is likely one of the few State capital buildings left with such ease of access and a foot placed firmly in the past. When compared to modern city halls, like the concrete monstrosity that is home to Boston's city government, the small elevators and gilded trim of the portraits in the halls are welcoming.

Visitor Information

Providence City Hall is open Monday through Friday. For more details about the building or offices please dial 401-421-7740. Visiting is encouraged and the staff more than willing to help.

3 The Biltmore Hotel

11 Dorrance Street

Next to the city hall is another allegedly haunted location: the Biltmore Hotel. According to the hotel's web page the same architectural firm behind New York City's Grand Central Station, Warren & Wetmore, is responsible for another throwback to a different time. That different time included a speakeasy (illegal bar) being run on the premises during Prohibition according to the January 2015 edition of *Rhode Island Monthly,* which also mentions numerous guests having supernatural experiences in the rooms and halls of the early twentieth-century-era building. The same article offers a theory that some of the unsavory patrons of the speakeasy may still be there, in spirit, nearly a century after the last illegal drinks were poured.

A former guest by the name of Jack Stephens posted a video to YouTube of his stay in room 1102 of the Biltmore where he recorded a door slamming shut. The same poster uploaded a video of lights turning off and on in the same room along with a swinging chandelier. He states that he was alone in the room at the time when the repeatedly slamming door kept him awake into the early hours. The videos add some credence to *East Side Monthly's* December 13, 2013, edition claiming that the Biltmore was named the most haunted hotel in America.

Whether the ghosts are normal bumps in the night, such as air conditioning systems turning on or air in pipes, or something more than natural, such as a ghost of former drinkers of homemade alcohol, the hotel is a beautiful building, and the lobby has been turned into a semi-museum of photos of storm damage from the '38 and '54 hurricanes, as well as postcards and photographs of the time when business travelers stayed at one of the few hotels that offered each guest a view of the surrounding streets or plaza. The rooms with exposure to natural light may be one of the attractions that keep guests coming back and keeps some guests from allegedly leaving. The neon sign on the roof when combined with the uniformed valets and front desk staff contribute to the throwback feel of the premises and is a welcomed change from the generic feel of other hotels.

One of the former residents of the hotel, Mayor Vincent "Buddy" Cianci, claims responsibility for the ice-skating rink on the west side of Kennedy Plaza, now sponsored by a Rhode Island jewelry manufacturer. In true New England fashion, the rink goes by a couple of names, The Alex & Ani City Center and The Providence Rink, and boasts of being twice the size of New York City's Rockefeller Center's ice rink and hosts events year-round. The rink and the area west of Kennedy Plaza is one of the "blurred" parts of the tour. It has changed dramatically in the last twenty years and anyone with a copy of *Lovecraft's Providence & Adjacent Parts* would be utterly confused as to the location he refers to in the book. The rink and area west of it used to encompass the old train station, which burned and was redeveloped into restaurants and pubs.

Some of the pictures in the lobby of the Biltmore show this area under several feet of water after the Hurricane of 1938 and some ships have actually been stranded as far as the corner of Dorrance and Westminster Streets, according to Beckwith's book. A hurricane barrier was erected in the mid-twentieth century, and can be viewed later along the tour, to prevent the periodic flooding of downtown.

Visitor Information

Guests are always welcome. For reservations or more information about the hotel, a visit to their web site is strongly encouraged. www.providencebiltmore.com.

4 The Westminster Arcade

65 Weybosset, between Weybosset and Westminster Streets

Walk southeast on Dorrance Street, then turn left on Westminster, as long as there are no stranded ships obstructing the path, and look for the granite columns and peaked roof of the Providence Arcade, also known as the Westminster Arcade because of one of the two streets it rests on, which has been plagued by more economic woes than natural ones over the decades, forcing it to close numerous times. Today, the ground floor once again houses restaurants and boutique shops while the upper levels have been converted into quaint apartments.

One of the features of the arcade that has changed little is the immense atrium with a glass roof that allows natural light to filter down to the thirteen-foot-wide main floor. The smiling clerks, marble features, and glass front doors and windows on the shops seem to be almost a defiant gesture against the anchor stores and franchise restaurants the Providence Place Mall nearby has to offer.

The National Register of Historical Places Inventory Nomination Form, which was filled out for registering the significance of the arcade mentions the numerous fine examples of Greek revival architecture in Rhode Island, and this is certainly one of the best examples. The same form offers the bare numbers and facts of the building as well:

Built of Granite Stone in 1827 and 1828 it fronts on two streets 74 feet on Westminster at the North and 74 feet on Weybosset at the South and is 216 feet in length it forms a transept or cross of a 194 feet by 42 T.I.

The two fronts are ornamented with recess Porticos 15 feet deep each composed of six Qrecin Ionic columns of 3 feet diameter and two square antaes and crowned with an Entabliture and cornice forming a Pediment, the whole night of the front Colonade is 45 feet from the bace to the Pediment.

The Roof over the entrance hall or avenue is covered with glass 32 feet in width by 188 feet in length the roof over the stors is covered with tin.

You enter the Portico by a flight of 4 steps running with the corner Buttments the entire length of the colonade.

The hall of avenue running through from street to Street is 13 feet in width the building is three Storys high there is 26 stors on each story making in all 78 stors.

The stors in the second and third storys you assend by two flights of stone steps under each Portico in each front.

The Corridors forming the floors of the 2d and 3d Storys are protected by a strong cast Iron ornimental ballustrade railing capt with mahogany and running entire around the interior of the Building.

Tape measures and lists of material used in the construction can't quite add up to seeing one of the finest, some say hidden, treasures in Providence.

Of all the oddities in Providence, one of the more popular ones is the Ottoman Warrior looking down on the intersection of Weybosset and Westminster Streets a little farther along the street.

5 Turk's Head Building

17 Westminster Street

Turk's Head. One of the more unique sites along the Providence tour. A stone memorial to a shopkeeper and the advertisement he had outside of his shop in the nineteenth century.

Shaped like a "V" so that it would fit snugly into the wedge of Weybosset and Westminster Streets merging, the sixteen-story office building was completed in 1913 and was the tallest in Providence up until the Biltmore Hotel took the title. Looking down from his third-floor perch is the visage of an Ottoman warrior, the Turk in Turk's Head Building, which is another testament of the eclectic styling that makes Providence a fun city to walk in.

According to *Old Providence, a Collection of Facts and Traditions Relating to Various Buildings and Sites of Historic Interest in Providence*, published by the Merchants National Bank of Providence in 1918, which also holds the record for one of the longest book titles in creation, Jacob Whitman was a shopkeeper from the late 1800s who kept a ship's masthead with the imagery of a Turkish warrior outside his store and residence near the same corner. It was a popular landmark but was moved after a flood and allegedly made its way to Alabama where a group of drunks mailed it to the state's governor one night in what must have seemed like a good idea after several drinks.

When the present building was erected, the designers took it upon themselves to place the sneering Ottoman as a homage to the shop and advertisement that was once on the same block.

Remembering that this was once the tallest building in Providence, it's easy to imagine a secretive society looking down on the city like medieval barons surveying their land. That imagery isn't too far from the truth.

The top floors of the building once housed the Turk's Head Club, a society of mostly Brown University alumni and students organized in 1912, which numbered approximately 600 members during its peak. The club's members represented people from manufacturing as well as the professional trades, such as lawyers and doctors.

The club rooms and dining were provided to paying members from Monday to Friday between the hours of 11:30 a.m. to 3:00 p.m. "Eating is a universal human necessity. But eating in a select company in such agreeable environment at the Turk's Head Club is a luxury" may sound like a fine review of the restaurant portion of the exclusive club, but it was actually part of the legal decision handed down in favor of the Internal Revenue Service who saw the dues paid by members as taxable. According to leagle.com, the case of Turk's Head Club vs. Broderick saw the tax exempt claims of the club as misguided and the club not meeting the requirements of a non-profit social club.

The secret organization had to provide all the details of membership requirements, twenty-one years or older with good standing in the community and must be known to at least two club's board of governors, in the case they brought to reclaim the taxes they paid on the $25 yearly dues owed by members under the age of thirty-five and $50 per year for members thirty-five or older.

The restaurant saw a loss of $5,670.17 during the period reviewed in the 1948 lawsuit but was not considered a purely social organization. The annual dues were considered taxable and members were less than pleased.

The club appears to have slipped into obscurity, but some of the custom-made china the club commissioned for the dining room still occasionally pop up on sites like restaurantwarecollectors.com or, one can imagine, the odd flea market or estate sale. The leering Turk's Head may not be the most appetizing imagery one could ever put on plates and cups, but they would make an interesting conversation piece if one could be found.

In a little under three blocks, ghosts, bootleggers, world-renowned designers, and secret clubs are all represented alongside baroque and Greek architecture. It is little wonder that H. P. Lovecraft would include modified references to all of those in his tales. Providence has a distinction of having one foot firmly set in the glorified past and the other placed in a more shadowy history as well.

6 The Waterfront

Memorial Boulevard to South Water Street Bridge

Heading east on Westminster toward the Providence River, visitors will see College Street Bridge, the approximate location of the first bridge that connected present-day College Hill on the far side of the river with the center of the city. The first bridge, according to a plaque nearby, was constructed in 1660 and was repeatedly washed away. Some pioneering residents simply waded across the river at low tide when bridges were scarce and their business brought them to the hills rising up the opposite banks.

In the early twentieth century, this area was the home of numerous ships and warehouses. Moorings would be used by ferries running down Narragansett Bay to New York as well as ocean-going vessels leaving or returning from Africa or the Caribbean Islands. This is also the area that saw H. P. Lovecraft board ferries running down the aquatic middle of his home state as a cheap, simple way to battle the heat of New England summers. Today's river traffic is restricted mostly to the gondolas that ferry passengers up the river and below the numerous bridges.

Walking south along Memorial Boulevard, with the river to your left, it's hard to imagine that this area was once covered over in the name of progress. From the bottom of Weybosset to College Hill was once one of the widest bridges in the world, built to accommodate mostly parking and some buildings for the working community of downtown. Fortunately, the bridge was torn down and the Providence River was again exposed, and walkways and parks were constructed to secure the area from economic development.

One such park is the Irish Famine Memorial, which was dedicated in 2007. The park and walkway make up the lower southwestern side of the river bank and is a popular spot in the warmer months. It is not uncommon to see someone casting a line into the water hoping for a bite or several students from any one of the numerous colleges downtown soaking up some sun along with their assigned reading.

Crossing the river is required and the best spot to do that is on the South Water Street Bridge. Looking north, people can see the old and the new of Providence; office buildings to the left and older brick work to the right. Turning around, facing south, walkers can see the concrete feat that has perhaps preserved the view north: the Fox Point Hurricane Barrier. Large, concrete slabs can be lowered and large steel barriers swung into place in a matter of hours to keep the downtown area from seeing a repeat of the numerous floods Providence has endured in its time.

Crossing the street and entering one of the parks on the east bank, the most prominent feature is the gold and tarnished copper top to 86 South Main Street. The plaque out front identifies it as a bank, the locked doors imply it's abandoned, and the lack of weather damage hints that someone may one day open it up again. Some of the proposals for its use have included a Native American Museum as well as numerous suggestions for turning it into a restaurant. One can only hope that some enterprising soul will one day open the doors wide to visitors or diners and showcase the, no doubt, gorgeous interior. Until that day, visitors will have to settle for exterior views and pictures.

Turning left, visitors can see the first direct link to H. P. Lovecraft's writing on the tour: 50 South Main Street.

7 Home of Joseph Brown

50 South Main Street

Joseph Brown House

Heading left, or north, on South Main, visitors will reach the first direct link to H. P. Lovecraft's writing on the tour: The colonial era red brick building at 50 South Main Street was once the home of an alleged Son of Liberty, the secretive organization that organized protests against British rule before the American Revolution, related to one of the rumored ring leaders of the burning of the HMS *Gaspee*, a British warship that ran down smugglers in Narragansett Bay and, according to Lovecraft, had a hand in the death of Joseph Curwen, the madman in "The Case of Charles Dexter Ward" who was searching for, and found, eternal life.

The blend of fact, Joseph Brown being connected to the Sons of Liberty and their attack on the HMS *Gaspee* and Lovecraft's placement of the historical figure at the raid on Joseph Curwen's farm and destruction of the wizard/necromancer's lair, is something that repeats through many tales in Lovecraft's work.

It is possible Lovecraft simply superimposed the *Gaspee* raid on his tale of raiding Curwen's farm in "The Case of Charles Dexter Ward," changed the names and locations but kept the general feel of clandestine raids and pacts of secrecy. The "modified reference" and others found in Lovecraft's work may be why there is an argument to the existence of cults and literary works that Lovecraft created. Is there a cult dedicated to Cthulu, the tentacle demon sleeping peacefully at the bottom of the Pacific? Was the Necronomicon written by a mad monk and can it be used to summon beasts from other dimensions? The debate rages on and is fun to follow from afar at times.

What *is* fact is that Joseph Brown had a fondness for natural sciences and lent a hand in naming nearby Planet Street, the base of which was where he set up a telescope and invited friends to observe the stars and planets. John Brown, the alleged member of the *Gaspee* raiding party may have had a larger house, the John Brown House on Power Street, which is now a museum, and been a cunning businessman and slave trader, but Joseph appeared happier with scientific pursuits.

The building is privately owned and has been converted to office space making a stop merely external. It is still a fine example of colonial architecture and makes for some nice pictures along the route.

8 Providence County Court House
250 Benefit Street

A short jump across Hopkins Street leaves walkers in front of the Providence County Court House, the prominent feature on the eastern side of the Providence River. The outside, with its red and yellow brick accents, draws attention to the shore along with its 216-foot central clock tower.

The Georgian-styled building with a forecourt and pillars overlooking North Main Street has been welcoming visitors, both willing and not so willing, since the 1930s, although it looks much older. It took four years to complete the seven-storied building of which tales of wrongdoing and alibis for most of the twentieth century have been heard. Rhode Island has a reputation for corruption and has even gotten the nickname of "Rogue's Island" for its affiliation with everything from slavery to rum running to government corruption. If there was a major crime in Rhode Island, likely the victim or the perpetrator spent some time on the marbled halls discussing what can and can't be done.

While a public building, people planning to visit the interior should consider the people there for business. Some of the visitors one can encounter in the halls, however, are not there of their own choosing and may not welcome tourists.

A more welcoming destination is across the street, a park dominated by a column dedicated to veterans of World War I. The memorial has been moved a few times with the final spot being decided only in the past couple of decades when the waterfront was being built up. Memorials to other conflicts have also been added over the years.

Diagonally across the street from the courthouse, to the north of the park, is a former headquarters of yet another secretive society that has branches around the world, but the building is now dedicated to higher learning.

9 Market House
27 Market Square

Near the corner of College Street and Main Street is Market House, which was designed by Joseph Brown, who lived down the street and is one of numerous buildings in Downtown Providence that have been bought and converted into teaching space by a university—in this case the Rhode Island School of Design.

Built during the American Revolution, the site is where Rhode Islanders followed in the footsteps of their Bostonian neighbors to the north and had their own little tea party on March 2, 1775, two years after the more famous one.

According to *Old Providence: A Collection of Facts and Traditions* published by The Merchant National Bank of Providence, the Sons of Liberty, who were a secretive organization of colonists fighting against British rule, burned 300 pounds of tea near here, then walked to neighboring shops and painted over all signs advertising the brew. Another beverage with a connection to the building is rum. According to the same book, workers and builders were paid in rum, presumably from Newport, which was capital of the distilled liquor.

Market House was also once a lodge for another secretive group that is still around today, the Freemasons, one of the numerous societies rumored to secretly control the world. With elaborate ranking of members from Entered Apprentice to Master Mason, according to Freemasonry.bcy.ca, along with passwords and hand signs it is easy to see why some people would make wild accusations about the society.

Internet access, groups, and publications, such as *Philalethes Journal*, which can be found at www.freemasonry.org, "The Oldest Independent Masonic Research Body," have helped clear misconceptions about such organizations, but in Lovecraft's day, it was likely yet another kernel of the mysterious that he raised into a fictitious society of occultists.

The eighteenth-century building was originally two stories, but a third floor was added near the end of the 1700s and it was, as the name implies, a market for produce and goods that served customers from Providence and College Hill and beyond.

One corner of the building has a bronze plaque that marks the high water points for the Great Gale of 1815 and the Hurricane of 1938, both of which flooded the downtown area and caused immense damage to the city.

This area also marks the approximate location of "Cheapside," where numerous shops selling varied kinds of wares, were once located. Ships would unload textiles and other products south of the area, and some of that same cargo would become merchandise in the stores. Ships' crews would mingle with the citizens of the city in the same shops and pubs, which were once lining the streets here.

Regardless of the backgrounds of the customers in the area, Hope could always be found.

10 Hope and Cheapside
22–26 North Main Street

Walking farther north to 22–26 North Main Street, pedestrians can see examples of the kind of store fronts that once welcomed customers to the area. Hope Block and Cheapside are the names of the two buildings that still welcome shoppers with immense windows—once the only way to adequately and financially illuminate shops during the day—wooden trim, and tiled entrances. While the wares on sale are likely different from what was offered to returning seafarers and businesspeople in the late nineteenth and early twentieth centuries, the stores still offer a glimpse of a time when natural light and opened doors and windows welcomed consumers and not the fluorescent lights and recycled air of modern chain stores.

Visitors are always welcomed in the stores and a few nods to Providence's most macabre native son have been spotted in the form of Lovecraft T-shirts.

11 The First Baptist Meeting House
75 North Main Street

First Baptist Church. Old New England charm in the middle of a modern state capital.

Another welcoming establishment is farther along North Main Street, to the right, or east.

Built during the American Revolution, the first gathering of worshippers met here in 1775. Prior to that, worshippers met outside during good weather or at the homes of fellow church members. The congregation today can link their forming to Roger Williams, who was banished from nearby Massachusetts for his religious beliefs and moved to present-day Rhode Island in 1636. The aversion to building a centralized meeting hall for prayers, services, and functions was because some members of the parish felt that it would be a sign of vanity, which was something to be avoided, but may have also been fearful of religious persecution. Moving prayer meetings from one house to another, like a person on the run, may have been considered a better idea than one large building, easily found.

The members of the parish may have been a bit surprised to see their formal meeting hall reflecting the designs, a steeple and church bell that other religions boasted of frequently. Baptists were a humble group, not prone to engaging directly in debate with less tolerable sects.

Revolutionary thoughts were in the air, colonies were trying to break off from British rule, and a group of outcasts, whose founding father was an outcast of outcast's one state over, were breaking with tradition and building a centralized hall that rose high into the sky for everyone to see. The days of meeting in farms and having to trek different distances each week were over. Now the meetings could be regulated and organized around one focal point.

This also paved the way for more interaction with other congregations. Debates of faith can now also include references to which church had the greater bell and steeple, which was and still is seen as a reflection of the members of the parish.

Overlooking the manicured lawn and pathways of the First Baptist Meeting House, on the Thomas Street side, is an original of a much more artistic kind.

12 Fleur-de-Lys Building
7 Thomas Street

In true "Let's be confusing" New England tradition, the building can go by any one of three common names: Fleur-de-Lys, Fleur-de-lis, or the much more pedestrian-sounding Sydney Burleigh building, which takes its name from the designer of the building who proposed the idea to architect Edmund R. Wilson, who was able to materialize Burleigh's thoughts in 1885.

Saying that the yellow, black, and stucco accents stands out against its plainer neighbors is an understatement. Between the wooden supports, the stucco was molded into designs reflecting everything from Greek goddesses to mischievous felines to grinning faces looking down on the street and passersby below. It seems that every square foot of the building was adorned with an image that struck the designer and architect at random.

It should certainly come as no surprise that this building with its eclectic designs and adornments was one of Lovecraft's favorites, and he incorporated the house

Fleur-de-Lys. Yellow plaster, demonic imagery, and fair maidens are some of the features of the building that stands out proudly on the hill.

and street into one of his most famous tales, "The Call of Cthulu." An artist in the story, H. A. Wilcox, was frequently awoken by nightmares at the residence, which led to his forming a bas relief of Cthulu, the tentacle-headed demon, and seek help from Professor George G. Angell, who worked up the street at Brown University. This is the same neighborhood where Angell died after being brushed up against by a sailor, likely from one of the ocean-going vessels that would have docked along the river nearby. In true "Scooby Doo" fashion the "death" of Professor Angell was mysterious and questions lingered about the cause.

Another story about the house, founded in fact, is about Bertrand K. Hart who was a literature editor at the *Providence Journal* and wrote a regular column for the newspaper in the 1920s. According to "An H. P. Lovecraft Encyclopedia" by Lovecraft expert S. T. Joshi, Hart read "The Call of Cthulu" and noticed that the artist in the story, Wilcox, lived in the same house he once called home. Hart wrote a letter to Lovecraft joking that he was upset that a former residence would be the backdrop to such evil and further laughed about sending a ghost to the horror writer's residence at three a.m.

Lovecraft, known for a strange sense of humor himself, penned "The Messenger" in response to Hart's feigned hurt feelings and supernatural threat.

To Bertrand K. Hart, Esq.

The thing, he said, would come that night at three

From the old churchyard on the hill below;

But crouching by an oak fire's wholesome glow,

I tried to tell myself it could not be.

Surely, I mused, it was a pleasantry

Devised by one who did not truly know

The Elder Sign, bequeathed from long ago,

That sets the fumbling forms of darkness free.

He had not meant it—no—but still I lit

Another lamp as starry Leo climbed

Out of the Seekonk, and a steeple chimed

Three—and the firelight faded, bit by bit.

Then at the door that cautious rattling came—

And the mad truth devoured me like a flame!

Despite referencing the Seekonk River and not the nearby Providence waterway, Bertrand Hart found enough enjoyment in the poem to publish it in his column December 3, 1929. Writers can be, and frequently are, a strange bunch.

Seven Thomas Street was intended as an artist studio and residence when it was first conceived and opened.

A little farther east along the street is an artist studio still catering to people looking for objects of beauty and wonderment, which also has a touch of Lovecraftian background.

13 Providence Art Club
11 Thomas Street

Art exhibits and shows are still opened to the public today at the studio that once hosted Lilly Phillips Clark's work. The name is not likely to be known to many, but she was an aunt of H. P. Lovecraft, and he attended her shows at the club. People are welcomed to visit the studio and tread the same floors that Lovecraft did, according to Beckwith in *Lovecraft's Providence & Adjacent Parts*.

The building itself, according to Providenceartclub.org, can trace its roots back to the late eighteenth century when the building was first built by Moses Brown for one of his sons. The art club came into the history of the building in 1886, and the structure was leased to The Providence Art Club in that year, making it the oldest in the city and likely one of the oldest in the country.

The website boasts that the galleries are open and "always" free to the public during the afternoon viewing hours. A walk amongst the canvases and other mediums is suggested, especially on days when the weather may not be the most agreeable.

Farther along at the top of the hill is the most haunted place in New England and likely one of the most haunted streets in America.

Visitor Information
Up-to-date listings of shows and exhibits can be found on the club's web page www. providenceartclub.org. They are opened most days of the week and the complete list of hours are on their page as well.

14 Benefit Street

The faux gas lamps, red-brick walkways, and numerous mansions and homes dating back centuries can certainly make a convincing backdrop to ghost stories, especially on overcast or foggy nights. Any neighborhood with this abundance of old world charm would certainly lead to a sparking of the imagination with spectral images being "seen" peering from windows and alleys and ghostly strains being heard down a side street or from a nearby courtyard.

Benefit Street seems to have an abundance of such claims from people of all walks of life.

Lovecraft based one of his best stories, "The Shunned House," here when the area was mostly abandoned homes and barely surviving rooming houses and inns catering to students and visitors of Brown University. In the story Lovecraft describes the street once being the home of numerous families with graves situated in the backyards.

Most of the graves, according to Lovecraft in his story, were moved to Swan Point Cemetery and other graveyards around the Providence area. In classic "moving graves" fashion, Lovecraft wrote that some of the plots were missed and some of the original settlers of the city and state may still be under the asphalt and brickwork of the streets and homes on Benefit Street today.

Perhaps these are the restless souls that have been reported wandering the street in the early hours of the morning. Maybe the first people to reside on Benefit Street are the "pale-bluish" faces that Charles Turek Robinson wrote about in *The New England Ghost Files*. Who knows what the story is behind the horse and carriage that was seen by a college professor and referenced by Robinson in his collection of factual ghost stories?

A couple of things that are certainly facts is that Edgar Allan Poe once walked the street as he courted a local poet, Sarah Helen Whitman. Sadly, they never had their day at the altar, and some people believe he may be one of the spirits that still haunts the street today. Ms. Whitman may be another of the specters wondering the street in the early hours second guessing her decision not to marry Poe, who died roughly a year after she broke off their engagement.

Another fact is that H. P. Lovecraft had his wake here at the top of Benefit and Thomas Streets. Just to the left as you crest the hill, 187 Benefit Street. Perhaps Lovecraft himself descends the granite stairs in the chilly pre-dawn hours to walk amongst the other spirits on the street or maybe it's one of the other "guests of honor" who were remembered when the house hosted wakes and not the Rhode Island School of Design students it does today.

The red-brick garage attached to the white house seems to have been an afterthought by the architects, but it is the alleged home of large basins, which were used to cleanse bodies before dressing and exhibiting in the reception rooms when the main structure was a funeral home. While the main house is now a dormitory, the garage appears to be dedicated to storing maintenance equipment and vehicles for the school.

One of their more popular haunts, when Lovecraft and Poe were flesh and a blood, is at 251 Benefit Street, the Providence Athenaeum, which is south along Benefit.

15 The Providence Athenaeum
251 Benefit Street

The Providence Athenaeum is the fourth oldest privately funded library in the United States, humbling Boston's Athenaeum by nearly five decades according to the library's website. The organization traces its roots back to the Providence Library Company, founded in 1753 by a group of researchers and avid readers who could not individually afford to purchase books and have them shipped from abroad to the newly established colonies.

The group pooled their resources, ordered books, and stored them in the Providence Court House until the collection, as well as most of the building they were stored in, was engulfed in flames. Other places of storage were found until 1838, when the present Greek-styled building was completed and the library moved to the shelves that hold the collection today.

The creaking stairs, cloth-covered seats, hard-back chairs at desks overlooking the main floor, and an antiquated card catalog appear to have changed little over the century-plus since the building first opened its doors to the public.

While the public is always welcomed during normal operating hours, borrowing from the collection is restricted to paying members. Everyone is invited to attend any of the Athenaeum's Salons, where presenters from numerous fields lecture on their chosen field of expertise, usually every Friday with a full schedule of topics displayed on the library's website, providenceathenaeum.org.

With rumors of ghosts outside its doors and a list of visitors that include some of the most influential writers of the macabre, people should not be surprised by some of the more unusual tales and customs at the library, but one tale may be the cause of the alleged wanderings of Edgar Allan Poe outside the heavy doors.

According to the institution's own dedicated page, which can be linked on its homepage, to abnormalities at the library, Fascinating Facts; Athenaeum Facts, Stories and Oddities, or the much more cerebral sounding "omniumgatherum," the stacks were the setting for Poe's courting of Ms. Whitman, the before-mentioned poet, who lived on Benefit Street. They would meet amongst the stacks and chat, perhaps hold hands when no one was looking, and when the moment overtook them, maybe a quick peck to the cheek as a sign of their mutual affection.

The stacks are also the location of the demise of the relationship. On December 23, 1848, they were visiting the library and someone slipped a note to Whitman informing her that Poe had broken his promise to refrain from alcohol. The relationship was ended and Poe would be dead the next year after crawling back into the bottle, leaving Sarah Helen Whitman to walk amongst the stacks by herself.

The intense relationship was commemorated in November of 1984 by the library when they hosted "Poe Bizarre," an event that saw a nineteenth-century-themed bazaar selling handmade stationery, silhouettes, and calendars. According to *Inquire Within; A Social History of the Providence Athenaeum since 1753* by Jane Lancaster, local actor Norman George's reciting of Poe's works was so popular that he was invited to expand on the work he did at the "Poe Bizarre" and present an interpretation of the courting of Ms. Whitman by Poe.

In 1987, Norman George was accompanied by Karen Lambert who played Sarah Helen Whitman and they strolled amongst the stacks reciting Poe's and Whitman's affections for each other.

A year later Lovecraft was honored, but as a one-man show put on by local poet and publisher Brett Rutherford who read from his work "Night Gaunts," which was accompanied by readings of Lovecraft's work and period music.

The athenaeum appears to host an event about Lovecraft usually around the anniversary of his death, March 15, making the library probably one of the few which puts the local author on a higher proverbial pedestal than Edgar Allan Poe.

Outside, on the Benefit Street side of the building, right across the street from the Superior Court House, is a now dried fountain that was once alleged to hold the magical qualities of keeping people coming back to Providence. The legend was that anyone who drank from the fountain was destined to return to Providence. Perhaps the spirits that allegedly stroll the street at night have taken the myth to a literal extreme.

At the corner of Benefit and College Streets, turn up the hill and keep an eye for the lot where 66 College Street once stood. This is where Lovecraft once lived and now hosts a different building, the original having been moved to a different location along the route. The present occupant of the lot is the Brown University Department of Philosophy.

Lovecraft aspired to attend the university but never walked the paths of the campus as a student. His legacy does live on at one of the libraries of the school though.

Visitor Information

The website www.providenceathenaeum.org offers details of the hours as well as any upcoming events that the library may be holding. Visitors, members or not, are always encouraged to stop by for a visit.

16 John Hay Library
20 Prospect Street

Across from the famed Van Wickle Gates, which are opened twice a year to accept students and to see them off as they graduate, the John Hay Library is named after President Lincoln's secretary and houses an impressive collection of rare books and papers related to alumni as well as famous authors.

One of the most extensive collections is Colonel George Earl Church's 3,500 volume collection "…largely composed of eighteenth and early nineteenth century monographs on Latin American politics, history and geography…" according to the library's web page.

Lovecraft's collected works at the library is nearly equal in number with the same site describing him as a "science fiction" author and refraining from adjectives such as "horror" or "macabre." The library's site mentions that most of the works were donated to the library after the author's death in 1937 and includes thousands of letters and essays along with some original manuscripts for his work.

Amongst the eclectic mix of collections, perhaps the one that is the most macabre, even outshining Lovecraft's work, is the anthropodermic collection: books allegedly bound in human skin.

Fans of Lovecraft will be familiar with the Necronomicon, tome of evil spells and capable of conjuring demons, being bound in the skin of less-fortunate bibliophiles. The practice was not just confined to demon summoners and occultists;

Fountain. The myth is that anyone who drank from the fountain was destined to return to Providence. The travel industry meets mysticism.

some medical text books, such as *De Humanis Corporis Fabrica* by sixteenth century physician Andreas Veslaius, a copy of which is also at the Hay Library, were bound in human skin due to a lack of other leathers being available. The skin used was sometimes from convicted murderers or people who had left no one responsible for disposing of their remains.

A May 22, 2013, advertisement for a Senior Open House at the library mentioned *Dance of Death* by Hans Holbein the Younger, a sixteenth-century printer who collected numerous images of gleeful skeletons playing instruments, leading people from all walks of society to their death. The advertisement specifically described it as being bound in human skin and offered it for viewing alongside an original copy of *The Birds of America* by famed naturalist Audubon.

Christopher Geissler, Librarian for American and British Literary and Popular Culture Collections, said in an e-mail that the library has been testing the volumes in the anthropodermic collection to determine whether they are truly bound in human skin.

The anthropodermic collection is not the only chance for visitors to witness skin bared for all to see; the Naked Donut Run is a Brown University tradition that is decades old and which leaves little to the imagination.

"Secret until moments before it occurs, the Naked Donut Run has long been a source of excitement, intrigue, and mystique for stressed students in libraries across campus," wrote Katherine Cusumano in her expose on the thirty-year tradition of nakedness and pastry: "The Truth Laid Bare: Naked Donut Run Sweetens Reading Period," which was published in the *Brown Daily Herald*, January 23, 2013.

Often done on the last evening of the study period, participants load up on donuts and presumably the occasional cruller, make their way to one of the libraries on campus, disrobe, and put the naked in Naked Donut Run, although the mobility is more of a stroll. The naked bearers walk through the stacks and pass out the sweets to unsuspecting readers. "Students who find their studies interrupted by naked runners are generally very receptive," said anonymous participant Rose *13.

"The look on their face really made the experience worth it," said Dorothy, another participant quoted in the article.

"The Naked Donut Run is not conducive to a large crowd" Levi *13, yet another participant who wished to remain anonymous for the article, is quoted as saying. People expecting hordes of college co-eds streaking through the halls will likely be disappointed. Those who enjoy a deep-fried treat, likely not so much.

Along the north side of the John Hay Library is a small grassy knoll with a plaque dedicated on August 20, 1990, the centennial of H. P. Lovecraft's birth, to the local horror writer and collector of odd knowledge. The first couple of lines on the plaque sum up Lovecraft's fascination with the old and apparent shunning of the new:

I can never be tied to raw new things,
For I first saw the light in an old town…

The silhouette on the plaque seems more Alfred Hitchcock than Howard Phillips, but it is good to see that the author has gained the attention from his hometown as well as the university—though his request to attend classes was declined—which he deserves.

North on Prospect Street is the same route that Lovecraft took when he returned from New York City and mimics the route that Charles Dexter Ward took when he returned to Providence. Cutting through Post Office Square, now Kennedy Plaza where the tour began, across the river, and past the First Baptist Church was the route described in the story of Ward's return and brush with the supernatural.

The route continues past the "…gleaming dome…" of the Christian Science Church with horse-shaped posts on the street outside. Farther along the street, at the corner of Meeting Street and Prospect, a stop in front of the Samuel Mumford House is suggested. This is the house that was transplanted from 66 College Street, between the athenaeum and John Hay Library, and was once Lovecraft's home. Today it is one of the few buildings in the neighborhood that is not affiliated with a university or college.

Farther north is Cushing Street. Turn west on it then look to the south to see one of the more unusual features on the route: a cannon sticking out of a patch of grass.

Visitor Information

If you plan to visit the library, a visit to their web page first would introduce you to collections they have as well as hours of operation: http://library.brown.edu/hay/.

17 The Cannon in the Grass
Cushing Street

The muzzle is buried deep in the grass and its history is lost. One can only speculate that it was lugged up the hill, likely from the docks that once lined the river below, and planted business-end first into the ground as a hitching post for horses.

It is either a fine example of New England ingenuity, using a device designed to breach the side of ships and forts to keep your horse from wandering away, or an extreme example of neighborly intimidation. Who in their right mind would want to argue with the person who has a cannon in their yard?

Regardless of how it got there or why, the cannon seems to be a permanent fixture in the neighborhood and will be for generations to come. Thick layers of paint and touches of graffiti provide evidence of the decades, possibly a century or more that the cannon has been resting in the soil. The lack of rust or other overt signs of corrosion leads one to speculate that it may be bronze or another metal prone to rust resistance.

Farther along the walking route is likely the largest tombstone in the state of Rhode Island and possibly New England.

18 Prospect Terrace Park
184 Pratt Street

Off Congdon Street facing west is Prospect Terrace Park, which was established in 1867. It's easy to imagine generations of families coming to the park and admiring the view of the marble state house in the distance, along with newer additions to the landscape like the Providence Place Mall and the high-rise hotel that connects to it.

Lovecraft was allegedly a frequent visitor here and benches and stretches of grass are often occupied by sunbathers in the warmer months along with people stopping to admire the view and skateboarders who seem to have no seasonal restrictions.

Centered on the ledge of the park is a granite statue of the founder of the state, Roger Williams. His one raised hand at hip level seems like it could be ready to rock to either side as a gesture of "hey, not bad" in regards to the state and city that rose up from the humble beginnings he started.

The statue is from the 1930s and was built as a part of the Works Progress Administration, which found employment for millions in the aftermath of the Great Depression.

Prospect Park. Beautiful views of the city and a nice place to rest on a pleasant day.

As a finishing touch to the project, the actual remains of Roger Williams were interred at the base of the statue in 1939, making the statue and arch technically a tombstone. Williams had been buried and dug up a few times over the centuries: first placed in the lot behind his family home, then moved to a tomb in the North Burial Ground, then moved again to the present location in Prospect Terrace Park. The inscription on the tomb neatly sums up the present state of Roger Williams:

> Here reposes dust from the grave of
> Roger Williams

It seems fitting that the founder of the state would be given such a vivid place to finally rest.

The park is also close to the home of Charles Dexter Ward, who may have been tempted by the "dust" of Roger Williams as well as another of the homes of Lovecraft himself.

After a rest to admire the view of the city from the park, return to Prospect Street by way of Bowen Street, which is near the north end of the park.

19 10 Barnes Street

North along Prospect Street, Barnes Street breaks off to the right. At number ten was the fictitious home of Dr. Willet from "The Case of Charles Dexter Ward" as well as the actual home of Lovecraft himself at one time.

It is an apartment building today and not opened to the public. One has to wonder if the present residents have an inkling of the history of the building and know why the occasional tourist will wander half-way down their street to gaze at a nondescript apartment building. One also has to wonder if any of them have seen the ghost of Lovecraft, which has been alleged to haunt the building today.

Turning back towards Prospect Street is a grander home, again allegedly haunted, which was the home of one of Lovecraft's most fleshed out characters,

20 Charles Dexter Ward House
a.k.a. the Halsey Mansion
140 Prospect Street

Facing down Creighton Street is the majestic mansion of the man who tried his damnedest to cheat death and failed. The red-brick mansion behind the black, wrought iron gates and fence was where Dr. Ward returned to from his trip abroad and dabbled in the arts of resurrection.

The old-world charm and affluence projected by the building has not been tarnished by being turned into office space for Brown University or one of the other colleges in the city. It is a private home and hopefully will always be one. Sadly, the fact it is a private home means that interested parties are more likely restricted to the sidewalk out front and won't have access to the walls and corridors of the home.

Like any good New England mansion with hundreds of years of history the home is allegedly haunted. Who haunts the house is debatable but what is not is the history of the builder and his son and their unique history.

The mansion was built in 1801 by Colonel Thomas Lloyd Halsey, according to *Old Providence*, after his service to the colonies during the American Revolution and his assistance with the founding of the United States. While fighting the British in the 1770s, Colonel Halsey went to France as "...the agent of the owners of the privateers fitted out by the merchants of New England." Sailing with a pirate navy funded by shopkeepers is another way to phrase it.

While in France he helped in the negotiations that brought French troops to Boston and accompanied them on their journey across the Atlantic. It is uncertain whether he learned French before or during the mission, but it was a common language in the Halsey home since his son, also named Thomas, spoke it along with Spanish.

Citing his fluency in Spanish and French younger Thomas Halsey petitioned the US government in the early 1800s to become a consul to Bueno Aires where the family import and export business also had a South American office.

The passing of the colonel saw the mansion pass on to his son, who left the mansion unoccupied for years while he enjoyed the nightlife of Buenos Aires—when he wasn't engrossed in the family business or diplomatic relations. That fondness for the nightlife led to a different sort of relation.

Young Thomas Halsey fathered a child while in South America and, upon his return to Providence, seemed to be less than pleased with fatherhood and, according to Simon S. Bucklin from Bristol who is quoted in *Old Providence*, "...lived for pleasure." Perhaps one of the more bizarre accusations of Mr. Bucklin was that Thomas Halsey had a fondness for terrapin soup to such a degree he kept the turtles in his basement. It's hard to be more Lovecraftian than keeping caged reptiles in the darkest corners of your family mansion.

A legal battle took decades in the Rhode Island courts as the heirs to the estimated $250,000 fortune wrangled for the estate and business. *Old Providence* doesn't mention the outcome of the case, only contributing more whispers and accusations to an old New England family's history.

From a piratical diplomat to a son who loved the night life, it's little wonder that the home is alleged to be haunted today and was considered a possessed building in Lovecraft's day.

Farther north is the corner of Olney and Prospect Streets where the tour turns to the left, heading towards North Main Street and Benefit, the allegedly most haunted street in America, which will be towards your left.

21 North End of Benefit Street

All of Benefit Street, in Lovecraft's day, was a bit worse for wear. Run down homes, cheap inns and tenements and it wasn't unusual to see an abandoned home along the way. Today, the homes have been restored to their previous glory, the sidewalks have been retouched in red brick in spots, although frost surges still make for a

parkour-like obstacle course as cracked bricks and drops and rises in the road and sidewalk can cause a few twisted ankles. Cautious steps are advised even on the best of days.

House and Dome on Benefit Street. Benefit Street has often been called one of the more beautiful streets in New England with its eclectic architecture and tree-lined sidewalks.

Benefit Street. Rumors of undiscovered family graves have been a backbone to the stories of hauntings on the street for decades.

Brownstone. Many of the family homes from the eighteenth and nineteenth centuries have been converted into office space by the numerous colleges and universities in Providence.

One spot where steps should be carefully watched is at 66 Benefit Street and the cemetery behind Hallworth House, a nursing home.

22 Episcopal Cemetery on Benefit Street
66 Benefit Street

Behind the nursing home, where elderly residents can enjoy the view of cracked tombstones and weathered trees, is a small cemetery that was allegedly the haunt of Edgar Allan Poe, Lovecraft, and probably a few dozen ghosts: St. John's church cemetery, which is now the headquarters for the Episcopal Diocese of Rhode Island.

Walking down the slate stone steps, over the earthen paths visitors can easily imagine masters of the macabre bending over to read the faded inscriptions of markers. Maybe Poe or Lovecraft took part in tombstone rubbing, a hobby that requires paper to be pressed over the stone and charcoal or other mediums to be rubbed over the markers to pick up an image.

One peculiar marker allegedly on the grounds proclaims someone's death was brought about while bathing. This is also where the protagonist from "The Shunned House" commissioned the placement of a marble urn in memory of his uncle, Dr. Elihu Whipple, who "melted" while investigating the cursed basement of a vampire/ghost's lair.

Another peculiarity is the placement of a nursing home, which overlooks a cemetery. Spending your autumn years viewing graves and trees that appear to be from a horror movie set may not be the best life decision a person could make.

Head back up the stairs and turn south, or right, on Benefit Street and you will come to the home of the person who was likely responsible for Poe's visits to the graves and may have contributed to his early demise.

23 Sarah Helen Whitman House
88 Benefit Street

In December of 1848, Poe and Whitman were scheduled to be married but a trip to the athenaeum farther down Benefit Street and the passing of a note to the bride-to-be put an end to the courtship and some theorized led to Poe's death less than a year later. Perhaps the best summary of the relationship comes from the tome with the superfluously worded titles, *Old Providence a Collection*

of Facts and Traditions Relating to Various Buildings and Sites of Historic Interest in Providence (With Illustrations!):

Edgar Allan Poe lectured in Providence, visited Providence, carried on his courtship with Mrs. Whitman in Providence, and if all accounts may be credited, left a part of his heart in Providence.

Sarah Helen Whitman was the romantic inspiration for Poe's own telltale heart when he penned "To Helen" and "Annabel Lee," and the Whitman house was the starting point on their walk to Swan Point Cemetery the day Poe proposed to her. Coincidentally, Swan Point Cemetery is the final resting place of H. P. Lovecraft.

While Whitman broke off the engagement because she was concerned about Poe's uncontrollable drinking, she didn't hold strong ill feelings toward him. She became a staunch defender of Poe in the years following his death and also penned a poem herself to the man. Part of her poem describes Poe and matches the modern image most people have today:

> Again I saw the brow's translucent pallor,
> The dark hair floating o'er it like a plume
> The sweet imperious mouth, whose haughty valor
> Defied all portents of impending doom.

The exterior of the home appears to have changed little over the decades, and one can still imagine Poe and Whitman sitting on the porch, sipping tea, and discussing each other's work. Allegedly, friends of Whitman disapproved of the relationship, as evidenced by the athenaeum's claim that Whitman was passed a note describing Poe's return trip to the bottle, and this may be the cause of Poe's alleged night-time walks on Benefit Street today.

According to Turek's *The New England Ghost Files*, Poe is just one of the ghosts that is believed by some to be wandering the area at night. Some people have speculated that the best time, "Poe Viewing Season," to see the wandering man in black is around Christmas when the couple were scheduled to be married.

Farther down the street is another home with a literary connection, this one more modern and parasitic.

24 The Shunned House

135 Benefit Street

Lovecraft was a fan of the courtyards off Benefit Street where he would sit and read or enjoy some fresh air after a long day indoors. Perhaps the small courtyard to the side of 135 Benefit Street, where his aunt Lillian Clark lived for a while according to S. T. Joshi's *More Annotated Lovecraft*, was one of his favorites. Did Lovecraft sit there,

Shunned House. The well-maintained private home is a far cry from the decrepit crypt described by Lovecraft in "The Shunned House."

looking at the peeling paint of the house and memorize the architectural details? When he visited, did he wander around the different floors mentally placing characters and objects, then devise a fictitious history of its plot of land and structure? Did he put pen to paper and write the dimensions of the home in a notebook and make a sketch of the stairs leading to the small yard overlooking the street?

There is no better example of Lovecraft's fondness for warping real history and lore in his works than "The Shunned House." It is almost a macabre love letter to the neighborhood written by a native to be enjoyed by unsuspecting tourists who will be left confused at where the lines of reality blur into fiction.

The story follows Dr. Elihu Whipple and the unnamed protagonist as they become fascinated with the series of deaths that have haunted the house over the centuries. On one dark night, they venture into the basement—exposed to the street now after relocating of the road decades ago—prop up some flamethrowers, which didn't arouse the suspicions of the neighbors somehow as they carried them down the street, and waited to see what happened.

What happened in the story was that Dr. Whipple was consumed by the spectral occupant, and the protagonist made his escape only to return later with jars of acid—which the neighbors showed no concern about—and a shovel with a determination to once and for all eradicate the denizen that had claimed so many lives over the centuries.

Lovecraft described the home as "Unlucky...There were no widespread tales of rattling chains, cold currents of air, extinguished lights, or faces at the window." This was the type of structure that people, including Poe according to the introduction of the story, walked past daily without noticing. The greatest terrors are often the quiet ones in plain sight, Lovecraft seems to suggest in his masterpiece.

Most of the opening chapter describes the house and neighborhood, including the Golden Ball Inn nearby, which catered to President Washington and other dignitaries over the centuries, and the rumors of family graves not being uncovered as the city looked to widen the street and moved what remains they could find to the North Burial Ground.

Another fact that makes the tale resound so well is the implication that the inhabitant that had been consuming people over the centuries was a vampire. Rhode Island had a vampire scare three decades before the publication of "The Shunned House" in *Weird Tales* in 1924, which is referenced in the story. Unsuspecting readers may think that part was untrue.

Mercy Brown died on January 17, 1892 and due to the time of year was kept in a vault because of the difficulty digging through frozen dirt for a more traditional burial. According to a June 2013 edition of *Smithsonian Magazine*, "The Great New England Vampire Panic" by Abigail Tucker, Mercy's body was examined a couple of months after her death and blood was found to still be in some of her organs. Her family was still suffering from a similar ailment that she'd died from and the conclusion was made that she was returning from the grave and "consuming" from her family.

The "cure" was to remove Mercy's heart, burn it, and mix the ashes with water, then have her surviving family member drink it to ward off the effects of the "curse." Her brother, Edwin, died two months later, likely from tuberculosis, referred to as consumption at the time, which is what caused the whole misconception of the dead walking amongst the living to feast upon their lifeblood and souls in the first place.

Similar events happened in the last few years of the nineteenth century and Lovecraft must have enjoyed hearing the different versions and whispers of undead hordes rampaging through unsuspecting villages in the rural western part of his home state.

In "The Shunned House" he brought the rural tales to an urban setting and fans have been stopping in front of the yellow-sided home since.

Farther down the street is another stop related to consumption of a more natural kind.

25 Geoff's Superlative Sandwiches
163 Benefit Street

This is a great place to end the tour. Tables, chairs, free pickles, and, as the name of the shop states, superlative sandwiches.

The shop has been in the same brick-lined, glass-fronted shop writing out their menu in chalk since before Henry L. P. Beckwith first wrote *Lovecraft's Providence and Adjacent Places* in the 1970s. It is a local institution that dedicates its sandwiches to other institutions in the state.

Sandwiches have been named after local politicians, like Patrick Kennedy (cold turkey, hot pastrami, and the customer's choice of melted cheese) philanthropists, such as Alan Shawn Feinstein (hot roast beef, Swiss cheese, and mushrooms, topped with horseradish) who has donated millions to scholarships, as well as tributes to the alleged ties to organized crime that Rhode Island has become infamous for, The Godfather (hot pepperoni, Genoa salami, provolone cheese, and pepperoncini oil). Monsters have to settle for being represented by Godzilla on the menu (corned beef, Muenster cheese, spinach, mushrooms, onions, tomatoes, and a guarantee of dragon's breath)

There is a set menu at the shop but ordering one of the specialty sandwiches is recommended. One can get a chicken salad nearly anywhere; how often can a person walk into a shop and order a Margaret Trudeau (Canadian bacon, mushrooms and Swiss cheese)?

Lovecraft is not represented on Geoff's menu, but the neighborhood makes up for that shortcoming. In less time than it takes to finish any one of the sandwiches on order, a person could walk to a spot Lovecraft had visited or written about, often both.

It's fitting to end the day at a shop that takes the time to honor local celebrities and roguish characters by naming their sandwiches after them. H. P. Lovecraft set a fine example of that kind of respect in the tales he told when he name dropped historical figures alongside his characters.

Visitor Information

A Rhode Island classic for decades, the shop's web page has the hours as well as updates on changes to the menu. Bring your appetite. www.geoffssuperlativesandwichesri. com.

Other Spots to Visit

1 The Ladd Observatory

210 Doyle Avenue, at the corner of Hope

This observatory opened in 1891 and was a popular haunt of H. P. Lovecraft. He lived about a mile away from the observatory and would visit frequently, being granted access by a family friend who worked there. Lovecraft used his access to the telescope and reference library at the observatory to write some of his earliest works. He had a regular column on astronomical topics in a local newspaper and contributes his frequent use of the telescope to a back issue he suffered from into

Inn on Benefit Street. Visitors to Providence can opt for a stay across from one of the most famous homes in the capital.

his adult years. "So constant were my observations, that my neck became much affected by the strain of peering at a difficult angle. It gave me much pain, and resulted in a permanent curvature perceptible today to a close observer," Lovecraft wrote to Rheinhart Kleiner in 1916, according to lovecraft.com.

Today the observatory's dome is still there and functioning as the telescope is turned skyward at least once a week, clouds permitting. The surrounding homes and lights from the street may have an effect on the quality of the images, but the public is invited to contact the observatory and ask about public viewings.

The interior of the building is also a nice place to view. From the spiral stairs going to the roof and the telescope to the offices and exhibits on the ground floor, the building seems to have changed very little in the century and change since it was first opened.

Prior to GPS, satellites, and atomic clocks, time keeping was done by keen observations of stars and planets and their movements. Based on the expected time a given star would rise above the horizon, clocks would be set and the exact time would be recorded. Time signals would be broadcast and other clocks set according to the ink-stained scribblings of astronomers and their radioed proclamation of the time a star or planet was in a certain spot in the night sky. In a day of integrated circuits and digital watches, this may not sound impressive, but in a time when clocks worked on oiled gears and the observations of often overworked staff, it was a vital field. The tools of that bygone field are still on display, from models of planets and their orbits to an exceptionally precise mechanical clock, the Ladd is a virtual museum to a time when clocks and radio signals were a science required for proper time setting, which in turn was needed for commerce, such as coordinating train schedules, and other fields of science.

Ladd Observatory. When Lovecraft wasn't thumbing through dusty tomes of history, he was looking skyward and seeking extraterrestrial influences.

The park and benches outside the red brick building welcomes people to sit in the glow of the largest star in the sky and soak in the warmth. It is a nice little park where one of the most prolific writers of dark tales must have sat as well, catching his breath after a bike ride to one of the highest points in the neighborhood, likely at dusk. The flickering gas lights of the past have been replaced by electric lights, which may flicker on occasion but not by design, but the quiet grounds offer a bit of an oasis from the glaring lights and constant noise found in other parts of the city.

Visitor Information

Visitors are welcomed to use the telescope during the week. Hours, as well as a blog and list of special events, can be found on their website: http://www.brown.edu/Departments/Physics/Ladd/.

2 Swan Point Cemetery

585 Blackstone Boulevard

The cemetery seems to be a park of sculptures celebrating the dead and welcoming the living to a leisurely stroll. Privately owned, the cemetery was the destination of Edgar Allan Poe and Sarah Helen Whitman on the day he proposed to her. There is a now disused dock and flight of stairs on the river side where people would step off boats, climb to the grassy plots above and stroll, probably under parasols and bowler hats, and admire the white marble monuments celebrating the life of the deceased now laying below. The sculptured trees and bushes augment the statues looking down from pedestals making the place of the dead seem more like an open-air museum of marble and granite sculptures.

Visitors today come through the front gates at 585 Blackstone Boulevard and are welcomed to pop into the visitor's center for a map. Parking near the center is recommended as the cemetery is designed for strolling leisurely to your destination if you have one. It opened in 1846 and was one of the first garden cemeteries in the United States. It also became the final, final resting place of numerous people from other cemeteries in the Providence area when the prime real estate they occupied was needed for other things, like street cars and office buildings. Tales of family plots and smaller cemeteries being dug up and the occupants moved are a common thing in New England.

Resting amongst four Congressional Medal of Honor recipients, twenty-three Rhode Island governors, and numerous American Civil War veterans is the humble stone proclaiming the approximate spot of H. P. Lovecraft's grave. The granite marker has his full name, date of birth and death on it, and his proclamation "I Am Providence." It wasn't until 1977 when a group of Lovecraft admirers, according to the cemetery's web page, pooled their resources and bought and placed the headstone on the Phillips family lot. Regardless of the time of year, Halloween or anniversaries of his death or birth, there seems to always be a collection of trinkets left for the author. Coins, plastic figures of demons, and letters and poems are some of the more common items left. A nearby tree, that has been uprooted and replaced, was once the medium of choice for some admirers who would carve quotes from the author in the bark along with other phrases or images. The poetic vandalism wasn't admired by the attentive groundskeepers so the tree had to be replaced by the sapling that is there today. One can only wonder if a similar process will have to be done in the future as the sapling matures and its branches become thick enough to accommodate poems and salutations to the deceased horror writer nearby.

Perhaps the enthusiasm of Lovecraft's followers are to blame for the restrictions the cemetery has put in place for visitors. Photography is not allowed except with express permission from the staff, which may require a week or more to process. The gates are opened at eight a.m. and close at five p.m., but hours are extended to seven p.m. during the summer months. Please keep these restrictions in mind during visits and remember that it is a place of rest for deceased members of the Rhode Island community. The polite security staff that roams the grounds twenty-four hours a day will kindly remind you of any rules that may have been inadvertently violated.

Visitor Information

H. P. Lovecraft is just one of the famous people buried at Swan Point Cemetery. A list of all the permanent visitors can be found on their web page along with hours and rules regarding visiting. www.swanpointcemetery.com.

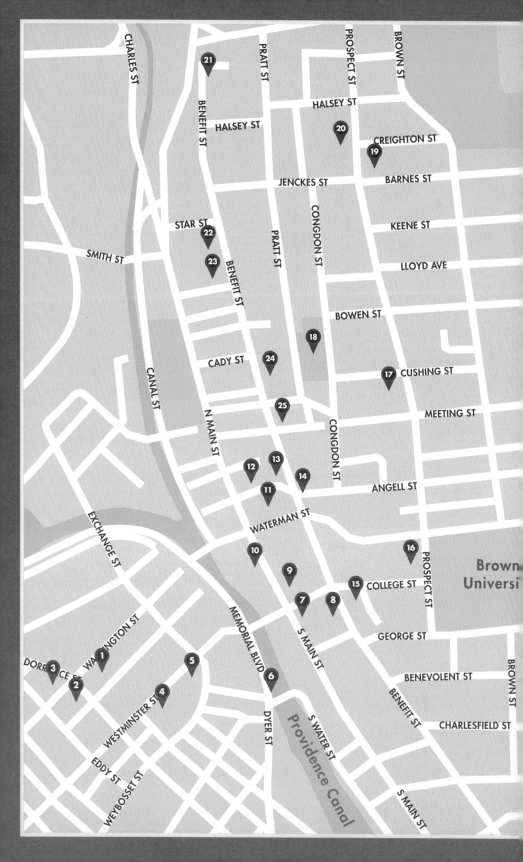

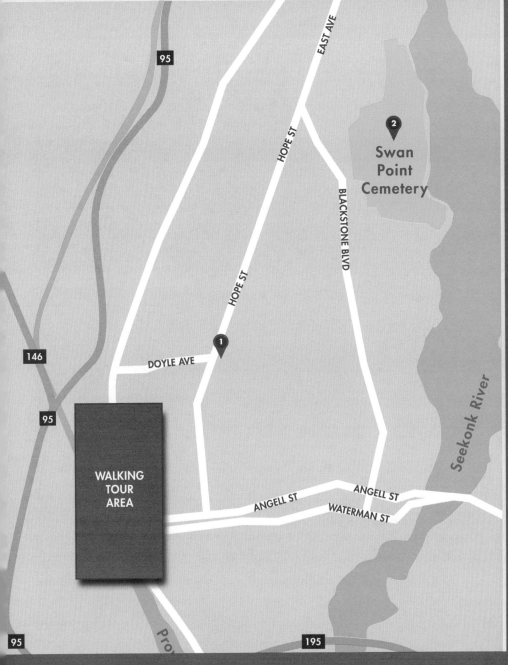

Providence Walking Tour Map

Prudence Island: Where the "Doat" Once Roamed

Ferry ride to Prudence Island. A pleasant trip and wonderful way to relax before taking on the trails of one of the lesser known destinations in the Ocean State.

Howard Phillips Lovecraft was a man of many peculiarities but one of his more socially acceptable ones was how he went about beating the sometimes dreadful New England summer heat. According to S. T. Joshi and Peter Cannon's *More Annotated H. P. Lovecraft*, the author of the macabre would board the ferry from Providence and ride south on Narragansett Bay, enjoying the cooling breeze as well as the view of the surrounding coast.

As Lovecraft rode the ferry from his hometown to Newport, home of pirate graves and spectacular mansions, he no doubt looked out on the passing islands and very likely set his eyes on Prudence, one of the largest in Narragansett Bay. He referenced a ship named *Prudence* in his masterpiece of the macabre "The Shunned House," and the name may have been influenced by the island he passed on those humid summer days. Did he ever step off the ferry and wander the roads? Did he know the tale of James Garland who fell in love with the seclusion and beauty of the island and built a mansion there, only to never use it because of tales of a paralyzing nervous attack? Was the island's "doat," a bounding animal that has been described as half-deer, half-goat, on the island at that time? To a writer of Lovecraft's genre, the tales would likely have been interesting and may have influenced a few novellas.

Maybe a fellow traveler interrupted Lovecraft's thoughts and told him about the village that was burned by its own residents to keep it from falling to the British as

Old dock. One of the numerous former docks on the shores of the island.

they fought their way to Providence from Newport. One has to wonder who Lovecraft, a known Anglophile, would have sympathized with in that story or the tale of the island's resident who assisted in torching the HMS *Gaspee*, the British warship that inspired residents of the state to rise up against the empire well before their neighbors in Massachusetts.

The still scenery of Prudence Island today can be explored by anyone willing to brave the half-hour ferry cruise across Narragansett Bay from Bristol, and the miles of, often, quiet roads and paths that make Prudence one of the best-kept secrets of Rhode Island.

The Walking Tour

1 Prudence Variety Store

837 Narragansett Avenue

If Lovecraft ever set foot on the island, it was likely at one of the other wharfs there, most of which are skeletons of what they were and resemble crumbling stone walls. The wharf that most visitors today disembark is Homestead where they can be greeted by the island's lone police officer assigned by the town of Portsmouth, which has jurisdiction over the island, and can purchase last-minute drinks and snacks at Prudence Variety Store.

The store is adjacent to the post office, which has a free lending library, and offers coffee and muffins for a quick pick-me-up. Printed maps of the island's trails and roads are also available for fifty cents, which can be augmented by directions from the friendly staff.

Besides the cookies, drinks, and directions, the shop also offers postcards, caps, and other touristy trinkets, such as cups and T-shirts.

One of the more unique postcards is the one of an albino deer, which was frequently photographed by residents, and was described as tame enough to eat out of some people's hands. Deer hunters, who visit the island during the winter months, were asked not to track the snowy white deer, which looks like a fawn in pictures.

The albino deer hasn't been seen for a while and some people fear that it may have fallen victim to hunting season, and there is a distant relative that may still be on the island but hasn't been seen in while as well: the Doat.

"Must be a Doat"
(Bristol Phoenix headline, September 26, 1996)

"Is it a deer or a goat? Must be a 'doat'" was the headline that greeted readers one day in 1996, confirming to some that the island had an unusual creature hopping along the trails and hills. The one known photo of the doat that accompanied the article, taken by Patty Richards, showed her cat, Rochester, barely dwarfed by the mystery beast as it bucks at the feline that was crouching ready to strike.

The doat was described as being trusting and occasionally walking up onto porches looking for food. Several theories about the origin of the creature are offered in the article ranging from a Dr. Moreau-like hybrid between a goat and deer, which is dismissed because the two species can't produce offspring with each other, regardless of how much they try, to the more likely, but far less exciting, theory that it may be an escapee from someone's farm and is actually a sika, Asian, deer that swam to the island, like the island's population of whitetail deer.

Sika are imported to the United States by some farms, and the theory of one escaping and swimming from the mainland, about a mile away, is more likely than a mad doctor splicing genes or confused deer and goat copulating in the woods, sadly.

The encounter and history of the unknown cryptid recorded in the article, which has no byline, was described as happening on an almost daily basis around Holbrook Avenue, which is north of Prudence Variety Store, along Narragansett Avenue, and is a good way to access one of the oldest sites on the island, the historical cemetery.

Visitor Information

Bucking the trend of having an Internet presence, the store can only be contacted by phone or snail mail. The telephone number is 401-682-1357 and the mailing address is 837 Narragansett Avenue, Prudence Island 02872. The Prudence Island Ferry service does have a web page, though, with a complete list of schedules and weather advisories. www.prudencebayislandstransport.com.

2 Historical Cemetery

(Portsmouth Historical Cemetery #41)

West of Alice Avenue

Head north on Narragansett, then left on Alice Avenue and then head into the woods that surround Portsmouth Historical Cemetery #41. Similar to many New England burial grounds, the cemetery has more than one name— Prudence Island Cemetery and Portsmouth Historical Cemetery #41—along with an abundance of oddities, a historical figure interred alongside unknowns, and a possible empty grave or two.

The main oddity of the cemetery is the collapsed rectangular tomb in the center, which may have gone decades—maybe even centuries—without repair. The occupant, if he or she is still there under the pile of rubble and dried leaves, is unknown and could pre-date the oldest interment, Mr. Joseph Sweet, who died in 1697.

Other damaged markers have developed legends over the centuries. The tombstones for Mr. Caleb Allin, 1723 to 1775, and Caleb Hill, date of birth and death unrecorded, were allegedly damaged by British cannons fired during the American Revolution, likely when British forces were sailing and marching their way from Newport to the head of Narragansett Bay.

Some of the oddest stones in the cemetery may be the duel markers for Joseph Knowles, 1760 to 1810. Another possible duplicate marking may be the stones for Caleb Pearce, 1745 to 1772 and Caleb Peairce, 1747 to 1772. Similar dates, similar names—which makes some people wonder if one stone may be a correction over the other and whether one of the graves is empty.

Amongst the anomalies is the grave of Captain Samuel Tompkins, 1726 to 1798. He was a farmer on the island and served in the American Revolution on the colonist side and may have been a member of the secretive Sons of Liberty, which opposed the British rule of the colonies and were responsible for some of the most famous acts of rebellion before the American Revolution, such as the Boston Tea Party and the lesser known burning of the HMS *Gaspee*.

The HMS *Gaspee* was, as mentioned earlier, a British ship that sailed Narragansett Bay intercepting smugglers who were bypassing stiff tariffs on products that the colonists felt they required for daily living, such as rum. On the evening of June 9, 1772, the ship ran aground a few miles north of Prudence as it was chasing a smuggler. It was boarded by local members of the Sons of Liberty, who shot and wounded the commanding officer of the ship, imprisoned the crew on shore, then burned the ship to the waterline.

One member of the marauders that evening was Aaron Briggs, who was living as an indentured servant on Captain Tompkins farm on Prudence Island.

Briggs was rowing a boat from one side of Prudence to the other that night when he was stopped by another boat carrying men off to the *Gaspee*, who were intending to attack her. Briggs stated in his testimony about the attack that he was forced to

Table and tree. Hikers are encouraged to sit and watch the waves and passing river traffic mere feet from the shore.

join the men on the other boat and was pressed into boarding the *Gaspee.*

Aaron Briggs was dropped off on Prudence after the attack and states that he went back to his room, which he shared with other servants, and woke the next morning and went about his chores.

Briggs eventually made his way to a British ship to, according to him, testify about the attack but was accused of trying to flee from Captain Tompkins. A sailor recognized Briggs from the attack, but Briggs was ready to testify against the organizers of the attack, naming names and pointing fingers at the people he alleged stopped him that night and forced him to join the attack. Anyone found guilty of the attack would have likely been sentenced to death.

Samuel Tompkins got involved in the hearings and stated that Aaron Briggs could not have been there the night the *Gaspee* burned because Briggs hadn't left the island for over a year. Who were the investigators going to believe, an honorable farmer or the indentured servant who was likely making the story up in a bid to earn his freedom?

The testimony of Capt. Samuel Tompkins was believed and no one was ever formally charged with the burning of the HMS *Gaspee.*

Today, the cemetery is in disarray and the marker for Capt. Samuel Tompkins has been knocked over. Hopefully someone has taken the time to reset the stone of the man who may have saved the lives of the organizers of one the first open revolts against British rule in the colonies.

3 Indian Spring

Southwest of the Cemetery

Approximately a quarter mile southwest of the cemetery is Indian Spring, at one time the only source of fresh water on the island. The first colonists on the island shared the spring with the local Native Americans, the Narragansett, and a circle of stones was eventually placed around the spring as a marker as well as mild protection from animals that may have wandered into it.

Reports of the spring being used continued right into the early part of the twentieth century, when plumbing became more common.

Today, the spring resembles a small park at the bottom of a hollow surrounded by towering trees and is a cool sanctuary on hot days.

Return back to Narragansett Avenue, which was named after the first recorded settlers on the island, and continue north. The Narragansett sold the island a few times but Roger Williams, the founder of the state of Rhode Island, changed the name from Chibachuweset to Prudence, for a virtue that Williams believed that all men should strive to achieve. Another owner of the island, John Winthrop, split the island between himself and Williams and went to work farming and building on the land.

Shoreline. The more typical rocky New England beach, the sandier one is on the southern side of the island.

The area north of the junction of Narragansett Avenue and Neck Farm Road is sparsely populated, has little development, and probably most closely resembles the marshes and forest that Williams, Winthrop, and other settlers to the island saw when they first arrived. (Note: This is about 3.2 miles north of the variety store.)

One such visitor from the early twentieth century was so impressed with the land that he immediately went about purchasing the entire north end to build a summer home but died under conflicting circumstances before he could enjoy it.

4 James Garland and His Mansion
59–63 Neck Farm Road

Garland Mansion. Over a century of standing, the mansion seems to be in a perpetual state of abandonment with some hints of life, such as windows and a manicured lawn.

In the late summer of 1904, James Garland was sailing with friends on his yacht, *Barracuda*, when they were forced to pull into Potters Cove, along Neck Farm Road and most likely named after a privateer from Bristol and one of the participants of the burning of the *Gaspee*, to wait for a storm to pass. The next morning, Mr. Garland went up on deck and viewed the surrounding land and immediately put a plan in action to purchase the area for a summer retreat.

James Garland was a graduate of Harvard University class of 1893, editor of *The New England Magazine*, an avid yachtsman and horseback rider, even writing a book on how to properly maintain a staff and stable. He was also worth several million dollars and had the money to spend to purchase the land. None of his publicly known traits contribute to the belief that he was prone to bouts of extreme anxiety or was in regular ill health.

Two years after pulling into the protective cove, James Garland would be dead, and obituaries would offer conflicting causes of death, with one even going so far as to describe the death as "...extreme nervous collapse."

Perhaps Mr. Garland was looking for a fresh start with his wife, whom he'd divorced previously, Marie L. Tudor, and he saw the seclusion of Prudence as a way to reconnect. According to the *New York Times* obituary from September 4, 1906, both Mr. Garland and Ms. Tudor were accused of "...overfriendliness with acquaintances." The same article states that Mr. Garland went about wooing her back soon after the divorce and perhaps she was on the yacht the night it anchored in Potter's Cove.

Pine Hill, comprising several trails over some of the higher points on the island, may have been where reunited husband and wife strolled hand in hand and discussed the building of the mansion up the road, which was built from local stones found in the field out front.

Maybe they laughed and got their toes wet in Potter's Cove, now the location of a dock for small craft and near beds of mussels and a weather station.

Maybe the thoughts of the couple were not so merry.

The most prominent feature on the northern end of the island is Garland Mansion and it appears to have always been abandoned. Mrs. Garland showed no interest in staying there after the death of her husband and there are records in volume 69, January 6, 1906, to June 30, 1906, of *Medical Record, A Weekly Journal of Medicine and Surgery* as well as *The New England Journal of Medicine*, vol. 154 that the mansion was to be turned into a children's hospital. Both were published before Mr. Garland's death.

In less than two years with $240,000 invested in the two story, thirty-six-room mansion (State of Rhode Island and Providence Plantations Preliminary Survey Report, Town of Portsmouth, 1979) it seems strange that Mr. Garland, who was ill, would have simply offered up the mansion on a whim. It's a bit of a stretch to say that Prudence could produce extreme bouts of anxiety to the point of a nervous breakdown, such as mentioned in the July 18, 1906 *Boston Evening Transcript* article about Mr. Garland leaving the island for the mainland so that he could be tended to by a family doctor.

The cause of death being called "consumption" at one point should be examined as well, since the term was commonly used in Rhode Island during the late nineteenth century to describe vampirism in towns such as East Greenwich and Exeter. After all, there is the collapsed grave in the cemetery down the road.

The only facts are sketchy and assumptions are not evidence. It can appear strange that a sportsman can become ill on a secluded island while being tended to by his wife, who accused him of "overfriendliness" with friends.

The case could also be argued that Mrs. Garland was so concerned for her husband's health that she rushed him away to another home on the mainland, likely to be closer to the family physician.

Junction in front of Garland Mansion. A re-purposed artillery piece from the old navy base on the other side of the island alerts travelers to the fork in the road.

The mysteries of Garland Mansion are like a Rorschach test: the viewer/reader can project what they choose to see. One may see a loving wife, begging her husband to abandon his investment and give it to charity as she pours him a cup of soothing tea. Some may see an additive to that hot brew that is not recommended for consumption. Others may see *consumption* as a synonym for *vampirism* and opt for the supernatural telling of the story.

The mansion still stands but can only be viewed from the public road in front, across the manicured lawn that hosts wedding parties and similar functions. A nearby farm is open in the warmer months and offers locally grown beef and is what passes for a supermarket on the island.

Farther past the bend in the road is a trail leading to Providence Point, the most northern part of the island. It passes the remains of some of the oldest houses on the island, basements of eighteenth- and nineteenth-century farms that have long been abandoned and have become part of a state park. These may be the remnants of the village that was burned by colonists as they fled before the British troops coming up the bay during the American Revolution.

As visitors stroll the paths and hills of the land once owned by Mr. Garland, they can enjoy debating which of the theories offered is true and will likely come up with a few of their own.

Not all mysteries can be solved, and those, sometimes, are the most enduring.

Islands sometimes require travelers to backtrack and Prudence is one such island. The dirt path that makes up Neck Farm Road is the only clear path back to the fork of Narragansett Avenue, Neck Farm Road, and Bay Avenue, which will be to the right as you head south and leads to one of the few well marked attractions on the island.

5 Pulpit Rock
Off Bay Avenue

Some historians believe that the natural formation of rocks, which resembles a church pulpit, was the site that Roger Williams used to preach to members of the Narragansett nation. Other historians believe that this is the site where the leaders of that nation, Canonicus and Miantonomi, carried out the day-to-day business of governing.

The sign in front only mentions the Roger Williams theory, ignoring that of Canonicus and Miantonomi, offered by the Prudence Island Historical and Preservation Society.

Regardless of which theory is correct—perhaps they both are—a modern visitor today should know that the trees that block the view from the top of the formation were not there at the time, and a person standing at the top may have been able to see for several hundred feet in front of them.

Heading back to the paved top of Bay Avenue, keep an eye open for a break in the woods near the shore and a small sign marking one of the better trails on the island.

6 Sunset Trail
West of Bay Avenue

As a person walks south on Sunset Trail he or she will have a stone wall to the left and open water to the right, occasionally obstructed by trees overlooking the cliff to the stony beach below. Prudence Island has some of the most stone walls per square mile in all of New England. They were used by the tenant farmers of the island to mark plots of land, and the simple, yet stable, construction testifies to the ingenuity of the farmers who needed to clear their fields of the obstructing rocks, which could break a farming tool, and found a way to use the annoyances to organize their fields.

A short way along the path to a walker's left is a break in the wall with a small, slate headstone and a larger, more recently added wooden cross and plaque. This is the grave of an unknown British sailor who washed up on the beach below in 1776 and was buried by the island's residents. Despite ill feelings between the Colonists and the British, the residents felt it proper to bury the stranger, who must have been wearing a uniform of the British Fleet since he was so easily labeled a sailor. The small plot of land where he rests is flat and one could easily imagine it being used for other graves, but this is the only recorded one.

Officially, this is the only grave on the trail but with lack of records, centuries of use, and times of sudden abandonment it's easy to imagine there may be a few other graves in the shallow forest overlooking the shore.

As one can imagine, Sunset Trail got its name for running along the west coast of the island and offering views of the setting sun in the afternoon. The designers of the trail, whether they were clearing a game trail or ancient foot path, took the sunset into account and set up some benches and tables along the way for hikers to sit down and enjoy the last light of the day as the sun made its way down over the city of North Kingstown. Silhouettes of pleasure craft and other ships and boats can be seen darting across the bay in the late afternoon, casting flickering shadows on the waves. Rustling leaves and branches accompanied by the occasional bird or skittering animal make it a wonderful place to unwind at the end of the day.

Farther down the trail, it breaks left and brings hikers back to the paved top of Bay Avenue and to the western opening of perhaps the oldest stone wall on the island.

7 Division Trail
Off Bay Avenue

While it is likely the oldest on the island, Division Trail also is the home of one the longest stone walls in the state. It runs nearly the width of the island, falling a couple of hundred feet short of the east shore and ends/starts closer to the waves on the western side.

The Prudence Island Historical and Preservation Society state that the wall was the dividing line between the property owned by Roger Williams and John Winthrop, governor of the Massachusetts Bay Colony. Williams had the lion's share of the property to the north while Gov. Winthrop had the southern half to himself. Both men farmed and raised animals on the land for trade and consumption and the practice was repeated by tenant farmers, like Capt. Tompkins buried in Historical Cemetery #41, over the centuries before the island became the community of summer homes and scores of year round residents it is today.

The trail today runs alongside the wall, occasionally crossing from one side to the other, over drops and climbs and meets up with School House Trail and Diamond Trail from the south. The west to east course is well marked by signs with the mathematical symbol for division, a horizontal bar with a circle above and below it, nailed to trees on the route making getting lost more difficult. As long as hikers maintain a course due east, they'll come across the paved road of Governor Paine Avenue and a little farther, closer to the east shore of the island, Narragansett Avenue.

Division Trail, like many of the other trails on the island, is maintained by the Prudence Conservancy Trail Gang which is made up of volunteers who clear the routes of brush and downed trees, make sure the signs are legible and check the benches and tables that dot many of the hiking courses.

On Narragansett Avenue, Prudence Variety and Homestead Wharf are to your left, going north. A worthwhile detour is a couple of thousand feet to the right, straddling the division line between north and south set up by Williams and Winthrop centuries ago.

8 Sandy Point Lighthouse

Off Narragansett Avenue

Heading south is the oldest lighthouse in Rhode Island, built in 1823 on Goat Island farther down the bay, and likely the only property "owned" by the president of the United States that doesn't require a check by The Secret Service to visit.

Since January 17, 1852, according to Lighthousefriends. com, the thirty foot tall octagonal granite structure has been guiding ships and boats through the eastern passage between Prudence and Portsmouth. The wedge of sandy land that it sits on juts out into the bay and the white tower with its black, bird cage

Sandy Point lighthouse and shore. The quality of the beach likely influenced the name of the jutting piece of land.

Sandy Point lighthouse. Originally located farther down the bay, the lighthouse was moved to its present location in the nineteenth century.

like top, has been the subject of countless photographs.

On quiet days, visitors can admire the view and take pictures until they are content. On days when the water is rough and the skies are dark, visitors may be reminded of the deaths of several people in the very area they are walking on.

On September 21, 1938, a hurricane struck New England causing millions of dollars in damage, flooding several cities, and contributing to the deaths of hundreds. Some of the deaths were in the lighthouse keeper's residence which was near the lighthouse and not as sturdy as the stone tower.

George Gustavis was the lighthouse keeper that day but was rescued by some on-lookers who were able to pull him to shore as a tidal wave rushed up the bay and engulfed boats, villages, and towns on the shores along the way. His wife and son were not as fortunate as they were dragged out to sea, along with three guests staying at the keeper's cottage. Not all of the bodies were recovered.

An electric light was installed soon after the storm making the lighthouse keeper's job obsolete and the automated system still functions today on the sandy stretch of land that gives the point its name.

Over the years other stories have been told about the lighthouse but perhaps the most unusual was an old deed that gave the lighthouse and the property it sits on to President Millard Fillmore, 1850 to 1853. The land deed stipulates that each successive president would become owner of the lighthouse, presumably contracting out the day to day duties of running it.

In 2000 the United States Coast Guard, who have a working relationship with the president of the United States, placed the care and function of the lighthouse with the American Lighthouse Foundation for twenty years. The islanders engaged in "...vociferous protests..." to the move according to lighthousefriends.com and today the lighthouse and surrounding plot of land are maintained by the Prudence Island Conservancy.

As hikers make their way back to Homestead Wharf and the ferry cruise back to the mainland the word "vociferous" is likely not the way they would describe the island of a mysterious creature, a figuratively haunted mansion, and sheltered trails and coves.

There are some homes that can be rented for a week on the island for those who would like to stretch out the quiet time in one of the least visited spots in Rhode Island.

Morgan McGinley called Prudence "A New England Secret" in a March 28, 1982, travel article for the *New York Times*. While the prices he quotes in the piece have certainly changed along with the number of yearlong residents one thing has not changed. He wrote "Prudence Island is not for everyone because it is so quiet." In an era of smart phones and constant bombardment of noise finding such a place to wander, wonder at mysteries, and visit historical places is sometimes welcomed.

9 The Southern Part of the Island
Off Narragansett Avenue

Walkway to the Bay. Evidence of one of the docks, used when the more common mode of arrival was in a row boat.

Many of the islands in Narragansett Bay have been used by the United States Navy over the centuries and Prudence is no exception. Up until the 1970s, the southern part of the island was used as a storage facility for ammunition, ranging from standard rifle and pistol rounds to the much more cumbersome, and destructive, torpedoes and artillery shells modern navies are more frequently associated with. While the navy, and the weapons they carry, are no longer common on the island, the bunkers and huts they once used can still be found today along the trails of the southern half of Prudence Island.

Prudence Island School House. One of the more recently used one-room school houses in the United States.

Most of the earth-covered bunkers are locked but some enthusiastic visitors have pried open the steel doors of a few of them exposing the well preserved concrete walls and wooden benches to the outside. The dirt and grass on the tops served a couple of purposes; one was as a natural camouflage, which made them difficult to count from satellite photos. Another, and likely the more practical use, was as a natural padding to keep any possible accidental explosions confined. The earth reinforced the concrete and timber that made the bunkers tough to begin with.

The farthest southern point of the island is actually T Wharf where the explosive devices were transported to waiting ships. T Wharf stands over the deepest water surrounding the island and hosted some of the largest ships in service as they were outfitted with weapons and explosives from the numerous bunkers on the island. Food and other provisions were also loaded up on ships which would make their way across the Atlantic or to southern waters during the hottest days of the Cold War. The seclusion of the island, which so many people find welcoming today, was also a welcome sight for the navy who wanted to make sure any accidents had limited effects on the surrounding area.

Besides the bunkers, approximately 20 to 30, the southern tip of the island also offers a sandy beach, which is a popular place for clam digging as well as seal sighting. The Narragansett Bay Research Reserve operates a park center on the southern tip today and welcomes school groups, as well as random tourists to the small center with displays about the local fauna and birds. A self-guided tour of the southern tip is also available at the center's web site, nbnerr.org.

Some words of caution about the island, in particular the south part of it. Besides the normal precautions against deer ticks and the potential of Lyme disease, hikers should also be careful if they choose to enter any of the bunkers which may be open. They were locked and were not intended to be visited. No guarantees about the condition of the bunkers and how safe they may or may not be can be made. It is recommended not to enter them, even if they are open and the metal door has been opened.

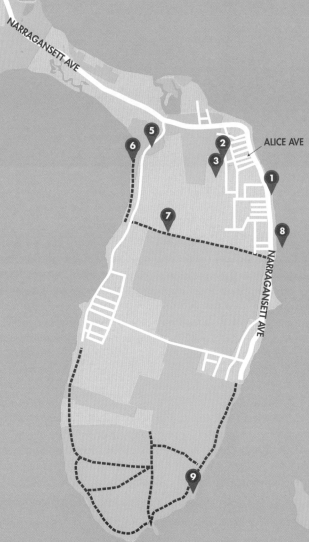

Prudence Island Walking Tour Map
1. Prudence Variety Store
2. Historical Cemetery
   (Portsmouth Historical Cemetery #41)
3. Indian Spring
4. James Garland and his Mansion
5. Pulpit Rock
6. Sunset Trail
7. Division Trail
8. Sandy Point Lighthouse
9. The Southern Part of the Island

Narragansett
Bay

NARRAGANSETT AVE

ALICE AVE

NARRAGANSETT AVE

Newport: Ghosts, Rum, and Mercenaries

Fort Adams. One of the largest fortifications on the East Coast, the grounds are open year-round and the fortress itself is a popular destination during the warmer months.

Newport, Rhode Island, has survived mercenaries, pirates, military occupation, judicial wrongs, and economic downturns since its founding. Hardship frequently contributes to the best tales.

Founded in 1639 by religious outcasts who were driven to the island by other outcasts from the Massachusetts colony up the road, Newport has always exhibited a unique blend of independence with a touch of criminality. Whether it was the contributions to the slave trade, smuggling of rum during prohibition, or the privateer, some say "pirate," fleets that tracked down and captured foreign ships at sea, the residents have a history of turning a profit from the misfortunes, illegal wants, as well as miseries, of others.

The centuries-old tradition of turning a blind eye to how money was made may be a contributing factor to why so many economic barons from the nineteenth and twentieth centuries found Newport a splendid place to build lavish summer homes, which have become the main attractions to the city on Narragansett Bay. Maybe they felt secure thinking that the locals wouldn't mind a cut-throat businessman as a neighbor, after all this was the same town that allegedly gathered in whole to greet "The Rhode Island Pirate" when he returned from a voyage. The oldest tavern in town, as well as the United States, once owned by a privateer, was the unofficial town hall and served as a courthouse as well. The city has a history of understanding alternative income streams. Newport also exhibited a form of crowd-funding, a century before it became common on-line, to build a landmark hotel.

Today, there are no pirates swaggering in the streets, but their history is remembered along with the Hessian mercenaries and British troops who once called Aquidneck Island, where Newport is located, home during the American Revolution. Some residents are still seeking profit in non-traditional sources of income, but of much more ethical varieties than some of the city's founding members. The history of colder sources of income are viewable and remembered today in the forms of drinks and plaques. Newport has some of the oldest colonial homes in the United States and a walk amongst the clapboard homes and along the ocean scented waterfront is a peek at a different time.

The Walking Tour

1 White Horse Tavern

26 Marlborough Street

Once the home of pirates and the drink most often associated with them, rum, it is only fitting to start a walking tour of Newport with a pint in hand, sitting at a bar that has seen everyone from construction workers down the street to politicians with ambitions of governorship, or even the presidency, walk through its doors. The staff and owners have changed over the centuries, but the eclectic clientele has not.

The White Horse Tavern's web page summarizes the regulars when the doors were first opened to drinkers and eaters in 1673, "…The White Horse was a regular haunt for colonists, British soldiers, Hessian mercenaries, pirates, sailors, founding fathers, and all manner of early American folk." William Mayes Sr. converted the farm building into a tavern and placed a sign with a white horse outside the door, which is an image associated with drinks and food at a time when not everyone could read, and welcomed people from all walks of life into his establishment. This was a place for drinks and food catering to everyone regardless of social standing.

Being one of the first public buildings in Newport, the visitors often brought their jobs to the bar with them. While administrative buildings were being designed, probably at one of the beer-soaked tables upstairs, and the bricks and beams being transported from Massachusetts or beyond, the first citizens of Newport made the White Horse Tavern the center of community business. It was, after all, one of the

White Horse Tavern. Oldest drinking establishment in America. Sipping Scotch by a blazing fireplace in the oldest bar in America is just one of the reasons The White Horse Tavern is considered a bucket-list bar.

first buildings in the young community and easy to find. The colony's General Assembly met here along with the City Council and criminal court which leads some to imagine drunken jurors and councilors deciding the fate of the fledgling community.

The White Horse Tavern is the rumored site of a bizarre, possibly spirit-infused, example of colonial justice gone awry: the case of Thomas Cornell who was accused of murdering his mother Rebecca on February 8, 1673.

According to executedtoday.com, Thomas lived on his widowed mother's farm and was financially dependent on her, which angered him since she had provided large sums of cash to his siblings. The animosity between Rebecca and Thomas was well known amongst the citizens of Portsmouth, a farming community up the dirt road from Newport. She called him a "…terror…" and Thomas allegedly called the death of his mother "…a wonderful thing…" Subtle passive aggressiveness apparently was not a family trait.

Rebecca Cornell's body was found charred in her bedroom after she refused to sit down to dinner with her family, and her son was the last person to see her alive.

Thomas Cornell went on trial for his life allegedly at the White Horse, which was a known center of government at the time of the death. Rebecca's brother, John Briggs, was called and invoked spectral evidence while under oath. He stated that he was visited by Rebecca in a dream and she said, "See how I burned with fire." Why the spirit of Rebecca Cornell simply didn't say if she was murdered and by whom is something one has to wonder about. The testimony of ghosts is a curious thing. In true colonial justice tradition, according to *Old Stone Bank, History of Rhode Island Vol. II*, Thomas Cornell was not allowed to defend himself against the charges, making this a case where the dead had a voice through a dream and the defendant was muted by judicial bureaucracy.

John Briggs took this dream as a sign that the death was murder and the body was later exhumed. A wound was found in her abdomen, but a weapon was never recovered. The "evidence" was combined with the known hatred that Thomas and his mother had for each other, and charges of murder were filed. Calling the evidence circumstantial is an understatement, but this was two decades before similar statements and "evidence" would result in the Salem Witch Trials. Colonial justice was a peculiar thing.

Thomas was found guilty by a jury of his, possibly drunken, peers and sentenced to death. He chose not to appeal the decision and was hung before a crowd of an estimated thousand people.

Thomas's wife, Sarah, was carrying a child at the time of the trial and execution. When the child was born, she named her Innocent, likely as a shrewd protest against the conviction of her husband on the basis of testimony from beyond the grave.

William Mays, who ran and owned the tavern at the time of the trial, passed on the running of the business to his son, William Mays Jr., who got a license to sell "...all sorts of Strong Drink" after returning from his pirating days, only contributing more to the romantic imagery of a rum-swilling pirate telling tall tales to a bar full of strangers. Perhaps as a nod to those days, the White Horse purchased a barrel of rum from Thomas Tew Distillery, which is named for a famous pirate with local roots.

According to the tavern's web page there have only been six owners of the restaurant and bar, at least sixteen percent of which were pirates, and the colonial-styled pediment doors, large fireplace on the ground floor, and clapboard walls have stood the test of time and culinary tastes. The clientele has changed from the common German mercenary and British officer wanting to drink away some wages to more affluent diners and drinkers who made the tavern a popular spot during the America's Cup yacht races in the 1980s. Today's guests are more likely to be celebrating anniversaries

White Horse sign. Before literacy was more common, shops advertised with simple images outside their doors. A horse meant drinks, and drinks were often associated with merriment and gossip.

and accomplishments in what the owners have christened a bucket-list bar, a place where people travel to just for the experience of sitting in the same rooms as rogues and patriots, warming themselves by the same fireplace that founding fathers and British sympathizers argued before, ordering from a menu that has changed, in rooms that have not.

The blend of history, both macabre and traditional, and great food and drink is likely what brings and brought people through the white-framed doors at 26 Marlborough Street.

Visitor Information

The oldest tavern in America has a virtual footprint in the twenty-first century at www. whitehorsenewport.com. Hours of operation, the menu, as well as a reservation form are there for the visitor to use. A well-detailed history of the pub is also included for those who would like to know more of its storied past.

Summer months may see clientele singing "Take Me Out to the Ball Game" instead of the slurred sea chanties from centuries ago as they wander in from one of the last great ball fields down the street, Cardines Field.

2 Cardines Field

20 America's Cup Avenue

The baseball field and stadium was named after Bernardo Cardines, who was a baseball player and casualty of the First World War. Prior to that, it was a simple lot of land at the end of a train line used for locomotives to spill steam water and other waste that accumulated over long trips to Boston and Providence. Workers on the Old Colony Line would pick up improvised bats and balls, draw out rough bases and lines in the dirt, and play until the sun set and balls and outfielders could no longer be seen.

Neighbors complained about the mosquitoes and other vermin that the stagnant spill water would attract. What they got was the treat of seeing baseball games played in the dried-out lot leading to semi-pro leagues, the building of bleachers to accommodate the crowds, who were looking for something to do on hot summer evenings, and finally, the construction of the green-painted concrete and wood stadium in 1935 to 1937 as part of the Works Progress Administration that stands at the corner of 20 America Cups Avenue and Marlborough Street today. You may not be able to fight city hall, but you can argue with the railroad and get a ball park.

Thomas Gannon's March 2004 article for *National Trust for Historical Preservation* details the simple beginnings of the field when it was used by workers at the end of a long day up to its present form where it is home to a collegiate summer league where players from universities and colleges show off their skills for crowds and occasionally major league scouts as well.

The homepage of the Newport Gulls, newportgulls.com, who call the park home today details more of the humble beginnings of the ball park and some of the peculiarities that players and visitors can expect at games. Due to the limited dimensions of the ballpark, which has been shoehorned into the neighborhood, there are numerous oddities to be seen, such as the dugouts for the teams being side by side, commonly referred to as *hockey style*. One can imagine that the proximity of opposing teams may have led to a few hockey-styled fights over the decades, but today's games are civil affairs, devoid of punches and head butts. The dugouts were also designed for smaller teams, meaning that less than a dozen players from each team can sit between games.

Along the right field line is a warehouse and any ball hitting it is considered foul. The ball park is rimmed by homes and heavily traveled streets making broken car or house windows a common occurrence according to The Gulls web page. Ground rules also take into account the surrounding trees, any ball hitting them resulting in the ball being bounced back into the park is considered an automatic home run. Fans have also found out the hard way that ground rules also apply to chasing foul balls into the traffic of America's Cup Avenue. They may have chased down a ball amongst honking horns and screeching brakes, but they will not be permitted back into the ball park after recovering their souvenir.

Visiting media are reminded before arrival that the press area is amongst the crowds of the 3,000-seat capacity stadium. People will be sitting all around them and play-by-plays will likely be interrupted by shouts and maybe profanities from excited fans.

Games may be called on the count of fog, which rolls in from the Atlantic Ocean, a block west of the stadium. The breeze from the ocean also contributes to more balls being guided to the right field than left.

These are some of the oddities that make a visit to the ballpark fun and remind baseball historians of tales about The Polo Grounds or Ebbets Field, where players had to compete with each other as well as the neighbors and neighborhood long before colossal ballparks became the norm and smaller parks disappeared.

These parameters are some of the details that Jeffrey Staats and architecture students from nearby Roger Williams University had to deal with when they tackled renovating the field in 2003. Gannon interviewed the architect for his article and cited the replacement of the bleachers by the students, who were not paid for their effort but gained valuable experience on working on stadiums, and how the sweat and labor from the dedicated team likely kept the park from turning into a parking lot. Numerous times, the City of Newport, which purchased the land in 1936, eyed the acreage as a source of income, in the form of providing parking spots to visitors and workers in the cramped waterfront of the city.

The park still hosts games today and the Newport Gulls have a winning record in the New England Collegiate Baseball League, winning several championships since 2000.

Walking across America's Cup Avenue, turn left, or south, and you'll have the famous Newport Waterfront to your right. Here, ships have been coming and going for centuries but most of the vessels today are less commercial than they were in the 1700s. Most outbound ships then carried cargo which was just as valuable as gold and was a bit more fun to have than any shiny brick.

Visitor Information

The history of the ballpark as well as schedules and events can be viewed at www. newportgulls.com.

3 Newport Rum and Rum Running

Perotti Park

Today, the waterfront is dominated by Perotti Park and the docks for the Newport Harbor Shuttle, which runs to Jamestown and Block Island during the summer months. The same area in the late 1600s and early eighteenth century was the home to shipping, which brought sugar to the colonies from the Caribbean and saw privateers and cargo vessels heading out as part of the triangle trade of alcohol and tobacco to Europe, textiles and more alcohol to Africa, and slaves to the Americas. Amongst the cargo being exported from Newport was one that has always had an affiliation with piracy: rum.

The imported sugar from the Caribbean contributed to the Newport rum industry that saw at its height in 1769 twenty-two distilleries, which made the city "rum capital of the world," according to Clare Simpson-Daniel from the Thomas Tew Distillery in Newport, the only rum distillery in Rhode Island today.

Newport rum is considered colonial rum, meaning it is darker and aged in American oak casks similar to scotch or whiskey and much like its grain-based relatives can be enjoyed neat. The distilling process contributed to the attributes, such as strong taste and percentage of alcohol, of the rum that gained a stellar reputation.

"The consistency and quality of the rum being made in RI [Rhode Island] was the key to this. With the vast majority of the rum coming from a 1 square mile area on the waterfront in Newport, it was difficult for distillers to compete with inferior rum and it was easy for the best practices to be transferred from one distiller to another," wrote Ms. Simpson-Daniel in an interview. This resulted in Newport rum being bartered as a currency in Europe alongside gold and other precious metals. Ships and crews routinely faced months at sea and water in wooden casks tended to become undrinkable after a while but rum and other alcoholic beverages could last longer, contributing to the imagery of drunken sailors with mugs in hand swinging from the ratlines. The drink that augments fruit based concoctions today was a necessity to crews who could be facing months at sea before arriving at a port with fresh water.

The sugar trade was going well in the eighteenth-century colonies, according to Ms. Simpson-Daniel, up until the 1764 passage of the Sugar Act by the British government, which imposed a tax on the import of molasses. The rum industry was hard hit and the distilleries saw their profits drop. "Due to the British occupation of Newport during the revolution, rum merchants fled their businesses. For 135 years the once thriving Rhode Island distilling industry lay dormant." The Thomas Tew Distillery was the first licensed distillery in Rhode Island in nearly 150 years when they obtained permission from the state to produce rum in 2006. "Naturally, the goal was to re-create the rum that had been world famous 250 years ago."

Another tribute to the past was the name that was chosen for the rum, Thomas Tew. He was called "The Newport Pirate" after his port of call and his battle standard of a raised arm with sword in hand can be found on the bottles of rum bearing his name today. There is a story that the entire town of Newport turned out for Captain Tew and his crew when he returned with looted treasures and stories of his founding of the "pirate round," a course set across the Atlantic, past the southern tip of Africa to Madagascar and India.

The docks of Newport also had another brush with the alcohol trade in the early part of the twentieth century during Prohibition, "the noble experiment."

January of 1920 saw the passage of the Eighteenth Amendment. For over a decade the sale, possession, and consumption of beer, wine, rum, and anything else that helped make the unbearable tolerable was outlawed. In true Rhode Island fashion of revolt the state refused to ratify the amendment, along with their neighbor to the west, Connecticut, and drinks were occasionally hidden from prying eyes and, in many cases, simply flaunted as a potent potable protest.

More than a few people saw a business opportunity.

Danny Walsh was a factory worker, according to a March 25, 2008, article in the *New York Daily News* by David J. Krajicek, who left his $5 a day job and contributed to a fleet of rum-running vessels in Narragansett Bay. "By yawning at the National Prohibition Act, it [Rhode Island] earned a reputation as the soggiest of the wet states."

Boats could run out past Block Island and pick up crates of alcohol, which could be bought in Canada for $8 per crate and sold for $65 in Rhode Island, from passing freighters according to *Rum War: The U.S. Coast Guard and Prohibition* by Donald L. Canney. This helped Walsh buy expensive homes and a horse farm while also maintaining some of the fastest boats in the country.

One of Walsh's fastest boats would become notorious for its runs, and some have argued that a vendetta was waged on *The Black Duck*, which had been equipped with two powerful, and expensive, engines to enable it to reach speeds of 30 knots, far exceeding the average 11 knots of the Coast Guard cutters assigned to stop the flow of smuggling.

On December 29, 1929, according to the *New Bedford Evening Standard*, *The Black Duck* had made a pickup of alcohol, destined for soon-to-be disappointed New Year's Eve revelers from a ship and was returning to Narragansett Bay when it was challenged by Coast Guard cutter *CG-290*. The request to stop to be inspected quickly turned to gunfire and the pilot house of the fifty-foot *Black Duck* was "Racked by Gunfire."

Jacob Weissman, John Goulart, and Dudley Brandt were killed and the lone survivor, Charles Travers, was taken to Newport.

The Coast Guard claimed they were trying to disable the craft by shooting the rudder, but an unexpected turn by the pilot of *The Black Duck* resulted in the cabin being lined up in the sights of the gunner, not the rudder. Whispers were made that the shooting of the crew was intentional and *The Black Duck* had flaunted its speed one too many times at coast guard ships, which had been left in its wake.

Charles Travers was taken to Newport Hospital where he was kept from his attorney for several days. "It was an unfortunate killing" Commander Chalker from the coast guard was quoted as saying by the *New Bedford Evening Standard,* "but rumrunners and all others on the sea must understand the law of the sea that requires them to heave to upon signal from Coast Guard craft."

The questions about the shooting and the handling of the incident was cited by numerous opponents to the Eighteenth Amendment. While it is a stretch to say that the one incident of *The Black Duck* led to the ratification of the Twenty-First Amendment that made alcohol legal again in 1933, which Rhode Island endorsed, there can be no doubt that a few people raised a glass to the memory of the lost crew of the fabled rumrunner, *The Black Duck.*

The crewmembers of *The Black Duck* as well as the sorry demise of Thomas Tew, disemboweled by a cannon in the Arabian Sea, lend evidence to the dangers and whims of misfortune that many sailors faced and, in some cases, still face today.

Visitor Information

Off the beaten path of Newport's sidewalks, Thomas Tew Distillery is still worth a visit. Hours and directions, as well as updates on what the brand is doing, can be viewed at www.thomastwerums.com.

One organization, represented along this route, offers assistance to sailors in the form of inexpensive food and lodgings as well as other amenities.

4 Seamen's Church Institute

18 Market Square

The red-brick, white-framed building at 18 Market Square, on Bowen's Wharf, stands out from its neighbors for numerous reasons. It isn't a shop selling sunglasses and T-shirts to tourists, nor is it offering acres of parking spots, like the hotels nearby, and the humble café inside is probably one of the last places in Rhode Island where a large coffee can be bought for a couple of dollars.

The white ship's mast with a fluttering flag outside the institute is a symbol of the old, precarious days of maritime work when a storm could disable a ship for

Seaman's Church Institute. People often think of Newport as the home of million-dollar yachts and extravagant mansions. It was first a seafaring community and some of the people who went to sea needed a little help when their ships were in dock for long periods of time.

months or a crew could be left stranded by the impounding of a ship and cargo. The need for a place for people in the maritime industry who have been struck a blow of misfortune is the reason the Seamen's Church Institute was founded.

The organization, according to their web page seamensnewport.org, offers affordable rooms for those in the maritime industries but have expanded that offer to all people in need regardless of labor background. A search for rooms off season in 2015 showed single occupancy starting at just shy of $100 and rooms for couples slightly less than $150. The rates in July were not much different. Rooms at nearby hotels frequently run twice as much and with similar amenities. The rooms have been offered to guests under distress for free as well as at reduced rates as a courtesy, and the organization looks at the rentals of the rooms to tourists as a way to offset the cost of the assistance they have provided. Guests get a room at a great rate and have the knowledge that their charge is contributing to housing those in need of a hand up.

While sailors have always needed rooms, they have also required food and beverage, and the Seamen's Church Institute has not overlooked that aspect of the trade. The Aloha Café offers great food and non-alcoholic drinks for exceptionally reasonable charges. Try finding a large cup of coffee at any hotel or restaurant in Newport for less than three dollars or a sandwich for less than ten (at the time of writing!). Proceeds from the café also help augment the cost of helping people who have been directed to the institute from the community. A reading room, library, laundry services, and showers round out more of the services provided for free and make the life of a landlocked sailor more tolerable.

On the second floor of the building, rooms are on the third, is a small chapel painted in 1930 that seems more fit for a European town than a New England seafront community. Images of knights speaking with priests, bishops conversing with maidens, and strollers engaged in debate adorn the walls of the Memorial Chapel, painted by Durr Friedley, according to the Metropolitan Museum of Art Archives, Durr Friedley Records 1906–1918. Friedley had spent time in Europe painting portraits and was no doubt influenced by shrines and chapels he'd visited there when he painted the chapel. The imagery may seem to be an anachronism when compared to the colonial-style buildings and ship chandlers shops that are more often associated with Newport, but some of the famous Newport mansions embraced medieval themes in their construction and design, and Friedley may have opted to display those designs instead of the nautical themes one would expect to see in a seamen's chapel. Regardless, the chapel is worth a visit.

Visitor Information

Hours of the café as well as availability of the rooms can be found at www. seamensnewport.org.

Leaving the institute, after a coffee or light snack, cross America's Cup Avenue—named after the famed yacht race, which hasn't been hosted in Newport in decades since the Australian team claimed the prize in 1983—to Queen Anne Square, which is a link to the city's colonial, British occupation days as well as bordering the site of a ghostly encounter that made the news as far away as Boston because of the unusual police attempts to capture the culprit.

5 Queen Anne Square

Thames Street

Newport was expanding, churches were being built, and the White Horse Tavern was becoming too small for all the gatherings that a city of seafarers and religious outcasts needed to have. Like towns in the other colonies, Newport resorted to town squares, which became the focal point of the community. Baptists could meet Quakers and welcome members of the Jewish community along with Native Americans in town for the day. Items could be purchased and bartered and sailors from any of the ships in port could wander in as well. Similar eclectic gatherings can still be seen today on the grass and stones of Queen Anne Square, facing Bowen's Wharf to the west and overlooked by Trinity Church to the east, but the gatherings are far less commercial and more relaxing.

According to a *Boston Globe* article from May 25, 2013, the grassy park on the hill was simply and blandly known as "The Hill" during the colonial years. It eventually became business buildings and bars up until the 1960s when it was revitalized into a park for the community. It was named after the Queen of England, who greeted and thanked William and John Wanton in England for the anti-piracy work they did in the new colonies against marauding French privateers who were raiding Narragansett Bay. The brothers later became governors of the colony, and the strong ties between Newport, Queen Anne, who served as monarch from 1702 to 1707, as well as England were bound. Some people have theorized that the anti-piracy work of the brothers influenced some people in town to turn to piracy themselves but across the Atlantic or in the Caribbean. Never pirate where you live.

Queen Anne also supported the Anglican Church, in particular Trinity Church, which overlooks the park, and "The Meeting Room" monuments that are scattered throughout the park were designed by landscape architect Maya Lin, who also designed the Vietnam Veterans Memorial in Washington, DC. Each of the three stone "rooms" resembles the sitting area in New England homes of the 1700s and offer stone benches for people to sit and relax.

The park and rededication have Doris Duke, a summer resident, to thank for the founding of the organization named after her, which helps preserve historical locations and contributes to the sites that thousands of visitors flock to each year. Numerous buildings and parks throughout the region are thankful to the Doris Duke Charitable Foundation for helping to create parks like Queen Anne and preserve others. The park also received an additional approval and rededication by Queen Elizabeth II when she visited the former colonies in 1976.

While the square only dates to the 1960s and '70s, the surrounding buildings represent a hodgepodge of centuries. Notably, the houses and buildings on Church Street along the north side of the square have a modern store front on the corner and the Cotton House, built in 1720, only a couple of hundred feet away. Another oddity on Church Street was reported in 1906 in the July 18 edition of the *Boston Evening Standard*, page twenty-one.

Calling the police for an unusual noise late at night is not uncommon. Assigning two police officers to investigate is a bit much, but asking them to sit in a house, day and night, in an attempt to catch the culprit is quite excessive. Luckily, the owner of the house was the Newport chief of police, and presumably there was no crime in the rest of Newport that summer that the officers could be looking into.

The tenants, Hugh Sweeney on one floor and Mrs. Sarah D. Muenchinder on another, complained to their landlord, Chief Horton of the local constabulary, about hearing raps that came in bursts of three or four. Mr. Sweeney, according to the *Boston Evening Standard*, went to investigate and came back with nothing. No mention was made in the article about Mrs. Muenchinder taking a stroll amongst the empty rooms looking for the source. When the culprit could not be found, accusations of ghosts were made and police officers were assigned "to ascertain the cause of mysterious rappings which have annoyed the occupants of a double tenement in Church Street." "Police on Trail of Ghost" was the headline, and Newport quite possibly became the first city in the United States to expect poltergeists to abide by noise codes. One can only speculate if the culprit would have been fined or arrested.

"The police say they [the raps] sound loudest at night," implying that officers were assigned day and night to the case. Despite the police presence and officers saying that they chased the noise from one room to another, no culprit was caught.

Chief Horton "...was as anxious as the tenants to remove the cause of the noises," and his duo of poltergeist-hunting officers came up with nothing. No further mention of the noises were made and one can imagine the chief was asked a few questions of a delicate nature at future town council meetings.

No address for the house was given, but it was described as being across the street from Trinity Church and the cemetery there. Maybe the noises were a restless spirit upset with something or someone in the house. Perhaps the raps came from a neighbor who was enjoying a mindless prank on one or more of the tenants. Or maybe it was a lone police officer looking for a relaxed detail away from the hustle and bustle of the docks in summer. Only God knows for sure, and Episcopalians say he can be caught up with at Trinity Church across the street and at the top of Queen Anne Park.

6 Trinity Church

141 Spring Street

Trinity Church. Once the sanctioned church of the British Army and Hessian mercenaries who occupied Newport, today's churchgoers are a friendlier bunch.

The congregation was founded in 1698, but the building itself didn't go up until 1726 and was influenced by churches that were common in Europe and especially England at the time. The Sunday gatherings were a time for the members to catch up on news from other parts of the town and surrounding communities, making the need for the area surrounding the church to be open so people could mingle after service and not miss any of the good gossip.

The tower, which would have been the highest structure in the area for centuries, was used as a beacon for people traveling to Newport for years. It was also one of the few structures that survived the British occupation of Newport during the American Revolution but likely because it served as the garrison church for the British and Hessian troops stationed there.

The white steeple and church has been the focal point of numerous photos over the years and in the summer and autumn months looks, again, over small markets that are set up on some weekends in front of its bell facing the bay.

Like many other New England churches, a small graveyard is on the grounds and visitors can often be seen walking amongst the tombstones and photographing the granite slabs and their inscriptions. Some people may be disappointed to learn that the church is not always opened to the public, but on the rare days that it is, a quiet stroll in the aisles is suggested. Much like the outside, the interior is simply adorned but a sight nonetheless.

Construction completed in 1726 certainly makes Trinity Church one of the oldest structures in Newport, as well as Rhode Island, but there is one that is older and may be a religious monument farther along the route. Or maybe it's a navigational aid built by Vikings. Templar Knights have also been credited with the construction.

It seems that everyone has been credited with erecting Newport Tower but the people of Newport.

Visitor Information

The website www.trinitynewport.org offers information about the hours of the church, special functions and a listing of Sunday services. During the summer, tours are also offered of the interior with a strong focus on the stained-glass windows.

Leave the church grounds and bear right to Mill Street, and follow it to the top where it opens up to Touro Park and the round stone tower at the center of numerous theories about who came first, the Vikings or the British. Or maybe it was the Templar Knights.

7 Round Tower/Touro Tower/Newport Tower/Old Stone Tower/Viking Tower/Old Stone Mill Tower

25 Bellevue Avenue

Round Tower makes sense because its round; Touro Tower is appropriate because that is the name of the park it is in. Old Stone Mill and Mill Tower enter the gray areas of controversy because some people claim it was never built to grind wheat or do anything else that wind power would be used for. No one seems to call it astronomy or navigation tower because that is far too controversial a name for it.

Newport was founded in 1639, and one of the earliest records of the Newport Tower (which it will be called from here on in) was three years later when the tower was used as a distance marker for dividing up some land. An old deed, according to *The Old Stone Bank History of Rhode Island Vol. I*, mentions the tower as a fixed point that lots of land was measured from. "The deed was correct and dated in 1642," contributing proof that the tower was at least as old as the colony itself. It also debunks another theory that the tower was built by Rhode Island's first governor, Benedict Arnold (not *that* one but a distant relative), as a windmill because he didn't set foot in Newport until 1653.

Other details that chip away at the windmill theory, according to the same book, is that there is a chimney on what would have been a second level. Powdered grains, which would have been plentiful in windmills, are also highly explosive and open flames were frowned upon for fear of being blown apart. *The Old Stone Bank History of Rhode Island Vol. I* hints at a tale of an unnamed tribe that populated the area and were driven out by the Native American tribes that greeted the first colonists from Europe. The unnamed tribe had allegedly excellent stone workers and some have credited the tower to them.

Other theories point to the windows designed into the structure. They line up with the sun on particular dates and some believe that the tower was a sort of

Newport Tower. There seems to be more theories about the tower's construction and purpose than there are shipwrecks and UFOs in the bay.

calendar. This coincides with the Portuguese Tower theory, according to redwoodlibrary.org, which has a page dedicated to the numerous theories about the tower. Portuguese sailors are also credited with Dighton Rock, in Massachusetts, which appears to have symbols related to Portugal. Did the Portuguese also stop off in the Newport area before the first pints were lifted at the White Horse Tavern, and did they build the tower as a way to know dates and set calendars?

Some of the more elaborate theories mentioned by the library include the Templar Knights, who may have made their way across the Atlantic on a secret mission, according to Andrew Sinclair in his books *The Sword and The Grail: Of the Grail* and *The Templars and a True Discovery of America.* Maybe Durr Friedley's painting of knights in Templar-styled armor in the chapel at the Seaman's Church Institute is a nod to this theory.

Perhaps one of the most romantic theories comes from poet and writer Henry Wadsworth Longfellow. *The Skeleton in Armor* is believed to be influenced by the finding of a skeleton in, yes indeed, armor about twenty miles from Newport in Fall River, Massachusetts, in 1832. Longfellow wrote his poem of a Norse warrior who takes his wife across the sea.

> Cloud-like we saw the shore
> Stretching to leeward
> There for my lady's bower
> Built I a lofty tower
> Which, to this very hour
> Stands looking seaward

Longfellow seems to follow the Viking theory of the tower, and perhaps his stamp of poetic approval on the Norse theory is why the word "Viking" is so common around Rhode Island today. From the Hotel Viking, farther along the route, to names of tour companies and dry cleaners, some Rhode Islanders seem to have embraced the Norse theory.

Regardless of which theory a visitor chooses to believe, they should come to the conclusion that the mystery will likely never be solved and that makes the park a pleasant place to sit, relax, and wonder about the generations of people who have set foot here before. No doubt there is an extraterrestrial theory floating around somewhere so a discussion about the possibility of life not from this world can also be enjoyed.

After basking in the quiet of the park, trekkers can take a left and head north onto Bellevue Avenue. Across the street is another quiet spot for getting away from the noise of the city.

8 Redwood Library
50 Bellevue Avenue

Redwood Library

Founded in 1747 and with an original collection of 750 books, Redwood Library at 50 Bellevue Avenue is the oldest lending library in the United States. The original room that housed the collection is still there and restored to what it presumably looked like when the doors were first opened to the paying members who supported the shipping of the first tomes from England, and other rooms have been added over the centuries.

Today, the Harrison Room exhibits ninety percent of the original titles that were shelved when the library first opened using the same arrangement of books by size, not alphabetically, that was common in eighteenth century libraries. The room itself has been restored to the best approximation of what it looked like, except for the storage of the antique publications, which are now behind thin wired grates. "This original collection represents the interests and inquiries of cultured, educated gentlemen of the mid-eighteenth-century," according to the library's web page, redwoodlibrary.org. Browsers of the shelves will notice an abundance of titles related to plants and gardening with some scientific books as well.

During the American Revolution, the Harrison Room, which encompassed the entire library at the time, became the officer's club for the occupying British Army while they were stationed in Newport. Many of the books in the collection disappeared around this time, presumably at the hands of the officers who took the titles along with them on their journeys and missions. In 1806, the library started looking for the books and realistically opted for replacement titles, not the original books themselves. Although there is a likelihood that one or more of the titles on the shelves may have made a round trip back to the shelves from which they were pilfered. Other visitors to the shelves and tables of the library took away less tangible influences.

According to the same site, Thomas Jefferson visited the library with President George Washington and was so impressed by the presence of culture that the library projected Jefferson "…began championing classical architecture…" for government buildings—the same style that is so prevalent in Washington, DC, and other

Redwood Library. Once the British Army's officer's club, the original collection was looted when the occupying troops were driven out of Newport. The library has been trying to re-create the library's collection for centuries.

government buildings from the early nineteenth century. "So it is that the Redwood Library is possibly one of the most architecturally influential buildings in America." The pillars and arched roof that faces Bellevue Avenue is the style that allegedly influenced the design of Thomas Jefferson's own Monticello Estate.

Other rooms were gradually added as the library's collection expanded to its present total of 160,000 titles, many of which are stored in vaults below the building. The Terry Reading Room was added and is primarily magazines, which was eventually followed by the Rovensky Delivery Room and the adjacent Van Allen Gallery that frequently houses a changing art exhibit often with a Newport or New England theme. Each addition was blended seamlessly into the original design of the library to a point where it is hard to see where the old ends and the new begins.

Along with the expansion of buildings and collections, the library has also collected other items over the centuries. Marble sculptures of everyone from the fictional Robinson Crusoe to the artist Gilbert Stuart adorn shelves and nooks of the library's rooms. Hanging from the walls are numerous portraits, including five by Gilbert Stuart. A portrait of President Washington hangs off to the left as you enter the Rovensky Room and is attributed to Gilbert Stuart's daughter, Jane Stuart, by the staff but is noted as being by an unknown artist on the small, brass plaque at its base. Gilbert Stuart is the artist responsible for the original, more famous portrait of Washington that Redwood's copy emulates, leading to the belief that his daughter was the artist behind the one looking over readers and staff today.

In one corner of the Rovensky Room is an example of the age of the library and its purpose of putting knowledge and needs of the reading community before the value of its collections. Behind a slender velvety rope is a single chair, which, for the longest time, was set out for anyone to use. One day an auctioneer from a famous auction house saw it, examined it, and informed the staff that the chair which has been used by visitors for decades is actually a valuable antique itself and suggested taking it out of circulation. Having a chair break under you is bad, knowing that the chair is a century old or more and worth several thousand dollars is no doubt worse. Newer, less valuable, but sturdy, chairs were pressed into service and the antique retired to its place of honor. This is one of the humbler tales that makes the library an enjoyable stop.

The library is opened to the public, although borrowing of books and materials is limited to members, and the friendly staff is always willing to chat about the history of the building and its belongings. Taking pictures of the interior is discouraged as well as needless talking and use of cellular phones in most parts of the library. A little time away from modern life, walking on the same boards as presidents and military occupiers, is a good experience.

Visitor Information

The oldest lending library in the United States has a very informative website detailing the collections they have, the artwork that adorns the walls, as well as the hours of operation. A visit to the web page is suggested before walking through the doors. www.redwoodlibrary.org.

Exiting the library and heading back to Bellevue Avenue, bear right towards the Hotel Viking and an example of the lavish lifestyle that Newport embodied in the early twentieth century. Some people believe that the partygoers from the 1920s are still at the hotel today enjoying the excesses attributed to the Roaring '20s, literally in spirit.

8 The Hotel Viking
1 Bellevue Avenue

Situated at the prestigious sounding 1 Bellevue Avenue, the Hotel Viking stands out from the smaller inns and hotels across the street, which seem to be overlooking the driveway, valet parking, and restaurant patio in awe and envy. It was opened on May 25, 1926, to a parade, fireworks, public tours, and parties. One can easily imagine that the prohibition on champagne and Scotch was ignored as a few smuggled bottles may have made their way from the nearby docks to the tables of the residents in the ball rooms and lobby of Newport's latest venture, built to cater to the needs and wants of business people and tourists who made their way to "The City by the Sea."

Newport residents felt the need for a glorious hotel to host people who may have business with the mansions farther south on Bellevue Avenue as well as other visitors. Bed and breakfasts and smaller hotels were fine, but lavish ball rooms, thick carpets, and marble-topped tables project a better, more affluent image than smaller establishments could put together. In what is perhaps the only crowdfunded hotel in the United States, shares were offered to the general public and sold out in one day. The money was put towards securing the land and building the red-brick façade that greets visitors today. According to the hotel's web page, hotelviking.com, "... Viking represented hope for the future in 1926, not nostalgia for the past, despite its architectural nod to Newport's colonial history."

The lobby appears to have changed little over the decades, from the now decorative wooden key board behind the front desk to the clock in the lobby with Norse runes for numbers, a nod to its name as well as possibly the tower down the street, and ironically now projects the type of nostalgia for a distant past that the first drinkers and guests were trying to distance themselves from.

There are whispers that some of those first guests are still around and not considerate of others and their want for peace and quiet.

"Guests who stay in the back of the hotel have reported being woken up by 'phantom parties'—music and laughter happening in the hotel's courtyard but no one is there," wrote Melanie Nayer for an October 12, 2012, article about haunted hotels and places to stay for Boston.com. Numerous people have reported sounds coming from the same area on different websites, most with "haunted" in their domain names. Whether all of the reports are the same incident or multiple people reporting similar experiences over different nights is unclear, but the long corridors, dimmed lighting, and rumors of parties that would make F. Scott Fitzgerald's jaw drop contribute to the spectral atmosphere that the hotel can project in the early hours, especially after a few drinks at the Top of Newport Bar on the premises.

The doormen would rather discuss any of the numerous amenities that the hotel has to offer as opposed to rumors of ghosts dancing and giggling the night away. They will probably ask you for a valet ticket or offer directions on your way out and a kind "come back soon" may be heard as you make your way back to Bellevue Avenue and turn left, towards Touro Street.

Visitor Information

Make a reservation or check out the menu at the restaurant on www.hotelviking.com. Dates of availability can be viewed along with a listing of the food and spirits on the menu. A history of the hotel is also offered.

"Phantom parties" may be a recent addition to the English language, but an older term has deep-set roots in the history of Newport: "phantom ship." Touro Street takes walkers back towards the start of the tour and is geographically between where the SV *Sea Bird* washed ashore and where it was supposed to dock.

10 The Phantom Ship SV *Sea Bird*
Tuoro Street

ohn Ross Dix wrote *A Hand-Book of Newport and Rhode Island*, published in 1852, and dedicated a chapter to beaches in the Newport area, including Easton, which at one time offered nude sunbathing in an attempt to combat ghostly white complexions. Easton Beach, as the name sort of implies, is east of downtown Newport, and any ships, today or centuries ago, would have steered clear of it because of the rocky shores that surround its sandier middle. Newport Harbor and all the warehouses, shops, and docks affiliated with it are to the west, left-hand side as you walk down the hill of Touro Street.

"Connected with this beach a remarkable tale is related which reads more like a romance than reality—nevertheless it is strictly true," Dix wrote.

On an unspecified day in 1750, people living near the beach observed a ship coming into Newport, a sight that was as common then as it is today. Instead of the usual veering towards the warehouses and custom houses in Newport Harbor, the ship proceeded towards the stretch of sand surrounded by rocky cliffs and shore that makes up Easton Beach. No doubt a few people assumed a problem was at hand and tried to signal the crew. A few people may have started to calculate where the ship may make landfall.

All signals, likely waving of hands and shouts, went unanswered and the ship continued its course to the beach.

"As silently as a phantom ship she approached the sands into which her sharp keel struck, and so gently that not the slightest injury was sustained," wrote Dix.

Onlookers soon became boarders as they scrambled onto the deck of the ship to investigate, and likely they intended to have a few words with the crew, who must have been assumed ill or incompetent. Numerous eyebrows must have been raised, and likely a few choice words uttered, when the only living creatures aboard were a cat in a cabin and a dog on deck. Assuming that even the most intelligent of canines would not be able to navigate a ship even at the orders of a lounging cat, luck was credited with the ship making it to the beach in one piece. Adding to the mystery was a report that coffee was boiling in the galley, implying that someone had been aboard recently enough to start making a brew. Or the boarders had interrupted the feline before it could get its morning caffeine fix.

One of the ship's long boats was missing along with all crew members born with opposable thumbs and the SV *Sea Bird* became a legend.

The ship was registered in Newport to Captain John Huxham and was returning from Honduras, having been sighted the day before by another vessel, who reported nothing out of the ordinary. Some people speculated that the crew may have abandoned ship when they missed the turn towards Newport Harbor and feared they were going to crash on the rocky shore. But the crew never made their way into town, and the missing long boat was never recovered.

A hundred years later a newspaper article put forth a theory that seems to fit but has been called fiction. The best fiction has a grain of truth and sometimes the truth can only be passed off as fiction.

In the October 11, 1885 edition of the *Sunday Morning Star*, printed in Wilmington, Delaware, a story titled "The Lonely Ship" appeared. It tells the tale of Captain Henry Seldan who found himself unexpectedly in Ystad, Sweden, waiting for repairs to his ship. He was told of an elderly American living in town and went for a visit.

Who he allegedly met was Thomas Hanway who claimed to be a crewmember on the SV *Sea Bird*. What he had to say was a confession of sorts to a fellow American seaman.

According to Hanway, he signed up to work on the *Sea Bird* and became friends with Jack Hensdale, described as "...a serpent in human form...." Both Hanway and Hensdale were verbally and physically abused by the crew of the ship, in particular one man identified as Mr. Rundell, to the point that they plotted to jump ship in the next port of call. Their fellow crewmembers informed on them and they were shackled in their off time and suffered more abuse.

One evening, "…twas a black night; black enough for any deed…," both Hanway and Hensdale were working on deck when one of the crew, the extremely abusive Mr. Rundell, was washed overboard. Mr. Rundell's screams were heard all over the ship, and both Hanway and Hensdale couldn't help—some may say they didn't want to. They claimed it was the foul weather to blame, but their statements were ignored and they were charged with murder. Waiting out the days before arrival in Newport, they were regularly taunted and told they would be hung. It was at this time that the accused murderers removed the adjective from their charges and the shackles from their feet.

They broke free and went about murdering the crew that taunted them for so long and began throwing their corpses overboard. Washing the decks of evidence, they steered the ship along its intended course and sighted Block Island, which they rowed to in the ship's long boat. They made landfall, split the cash that the captain had in his desk and went their separate ways.

The article has some inconsistencies; no mention of a cat, merely a dog. The incident is also dated 1760. Regardless of whether the story is true or not, it is an example of one of many "phantom ships" that still pop up today devoid of crew and raising questions about what is out over the horizon.

The ship was salvageable and was renamed SV *Beach Bird*, perhaps as a macabre joke about its history, and continued to sail out of Newport Harbor which is near the end of the tour in Eisenhower Park.

11 Eisenhower Park

28–32 Touro Street

Eisenhower Park is a wedge of greenery facing the docks and the Museum of Newport History, in the old Market House, and in front of the still functioning Newport District Court at 45 Washington Square. It is also the end of the walking tour. A statue of Commodore Perry resides on a column looking out to sea, where he made his name as a gunboat diplomat opening up Japan to foreign trade and fighting during the Mexican-American War of 1854.

Newport has always embraced its history and seldom glosses over the less-than-glorious parts. It's little wonder that the city, which was originally used as a prison ground for the first residents of Rhode Island, according to *The Old Stone Bank History of Rhode Island*, still boasts of its piratical past and blatant disregard for laws that a majority of residents saw as unfair, like Prohibition or the Sugar Act. Newporters also seem pleased with their macabre side as they talk about ghostly hotels and mysterious towers.

Popping into one of the neighboring pubs or restaurants is recommended. The White Horse is a mere block north of the park if you would like to look at the lunch or dinner menu. Along the way, wherever you decide to go, look around for plaques with the dates of construction for some of the homes and buildings nearby. Listen for tales of more infamous residents, both living and deceased. Newport is a vibrant little town with history that could fill volumes and likely leave the most experienced of travelers surprised.

Other Sights in the Newport Area

1 Fort Adams

90 Fort Adams Drive, Newport

When the British fleet first sailed into Newport harbor during the American Revolution they demonstrated the need for the community to have a means of defense. The earthen walls of Fort Dumpling in Jamestown, across the bay, as well as other fortifications put up by the colonists, were quickly overrun as were the streets of Newport and all of Aquidneck Island, which became a British stronghold. The British used the foothold they had in Newport to work their way north towards Providence during the Battle of Rhode Island and the colonists took notice and started planning for a way to make sure it wouldn't happen again.

Fort Adams was built as a massive fortification that would not be easily overrun, if enemy troops could ever make it through the cannon fire that would rain down on ships in the bay. The thick and high walls of granite with few openings were designed to be imposing and not easy to breach. It's these features which people have to thank for the fort being there today.

Built over several decades starting in the 1820s the fort was designed and functioned as the command center for all of the defenses of Narragansett Bay and saw service right up to the mid-twentieth century. What made the fort nearly impossible to take over also made it impossible to demolish. The thick walls would be almost impervious to any attempt to demolish them and would likely take longer to destroy than it did to build. As with similar structures all over the world, Newport turned the area into a park.

Tours of the interior are available during the summer months and the waterside park is open year round. Halloween is a popular time for visits as the corridors and grounds host demons and ghosts creeping out of darkened corners to scare guests. Some people believe that not all of the ghosts are seasonal and so easily crawl back into the shadows.

Usually, a few times each summer, the fort opens their doors late in the evening and welcomes paranormal investigators as well as tourists looking for something a bit unusual and maybe supernatural. The tours last a few hours, right up to midnight, and visitors with flashlights in hand are welcomed to wander the halls, courtyard, and staircases of one of the most complex fortifications in the Western hemisphere.

One of the manifestations that visitors may encounter is that of Private William Kane, according to Christopher Rondina in an October 26, 2011 interview with newportri.com, by Bre Eaton. Mr. Rondina is a self-described ghost hunter who reported unusual activity in a barracks room where Private Kane was shot and killed in cold blood by another soldier stationed there in 1819.

In an August 29, 2013 article titled "Life and Death at Fort Adams" for *Newport This Week*, by Jack Kelly, the same incident is mentioned and the shooter identified as Private William Cornell who was given an extra serving of rum along with the rest of the garrison on that fateful July 4, 1819. The same article addresses the theory that some of the spirits that may be roaming the halls are some of the builders and excavators who may have died during construction.

One of the more sensational tales of death at the fort is that of Mary Gleason, who was found at the bottom of a ditch one snowy night. She was engaged to be married to Private George Henderson, who was stationed there. Another private, George Carmark Cordy attached to the headquarters battery there, according to a January 29, 1925, article in the *Cortland Standard*, confessed he murdered Ms. Gleason out of sheer jealously at the engagement. The murderer stated that he had "…formerly kept company…" with Ms. Gleason, as the newspaper so delicately put it, and took matters into his own hands to end the engagement for good.

Perhaps Ms. Gleason is one of the specters that is heard or seen around the grounds late at night or early in the morning. Or maybe it's the lamenting spirit of the fiancé or the murderer himself, remorsefully condemned to the grounds for all eternity.

Likely the questions will never be answered but that shouldn't stop people from going to the park now, which hosts the annual Newport Jazz Festival as well as other events throughout the year.

Visitor Information

Fort Adams is listed as the largest castle in America and the web page offers maps of the trails around the park today. History, a virtual gift shop, and directions can also be found on www.fortadams.org

2 Cliff Walk

Parking at Memorial Boulevard is recommended

Encompassing natural beauty to one side and architectural wonderment to the other, Cliff Walk is one of the more unique treks in Rhode Island. It is also a controversial one as the paths cross over private property at times, and owners of multi-million dollar homes have to occasionally crane their necks around packs of T-shirt-wearing tourists to enjoy the view that they thought would be exclusively theirs to enjoy.

The trail that runs over the cliffs, some of which are seventy feet or higher, is attributed to deer who were looking for food, then the Narragansett tribe that was likely stalking the deer, then to the colonists who followed the trails in an attempt to salvage what they could from any ships unfortunate enough to crash on the rocky shore below, according to the dedicated website cliffwalk.com.

Homeowners along the route have not always been so accepting of people disrupting their views, and there have been walls built, rocks moved to block paths, and some of the owners have even gone as far as moving the paths to more dangerous routes around the cliffs. Not all of the owners have been so hostile. A few have erected bridges and tunnels for visitors to make their way along the route.

One of the more unusual sites on the path is the Chinese Tea House, which is near Marble House and stands out as an anachronism when compared to the other architectural influences that are in Newport as well as Rhode Island. It is just one of the many examples of eccentricity that can be found all over the state.

As the name implies, it is a Chinese-styled house with curved eaves and adorned in red and white tones. It is also a popular place for people to stop along the route, catch their breath, and take in the views of the water below and the surrounding area. It is a pleasant site for people to have their pictures taken and enjoy the finer weather that New England has to offer in the spring through the fall. Braver folks may venture out there during the winter if they so choose.

Forty Steps is another example of attempts to make the walk more welcoming to visitors. Where most observation spots are built upward to afford a greater view, Forty Steps brings visitors down towards the water so that they can stand closer to it and enjoy the view with the amplified crashing of the waves on the rocky shore below.

The three-and-a-half mile walk itself is estimated to take about two-and-a-half hours. The parking lot at Memorial Boulevard is also the approximate spot where the ghost ship SV *Sea Bird* washed up with its crew of cat and dog. Today, dogs are required to be leashed—good luck getting a tether on a cat—and the ghost ships and scavengers have been replaced with sunbathers and sun worshippers in the warmer months.

Visitor Information

Open 365 days a year sunrise to sunset is just one of the boasts found on www. cliffwalk.com. Directions, history, and rules for hikers are presented to readers of the page. Public transportation options are also offered for those who are not brave enough to take on Newport's vehicular summer traffic themselves.

FARWELL ST
FARWELL ST
AMERICA'S CUP AVE
POPLAR ST
THAMES ST
ELM ST
FARWELL ST
BRIDGE ST
CHARLES ST
1
2
MARLBOROUGH ST
AMERICA'S CUP AVE
11
THAMES ST
CLARKE ST
10
MT VERNON ST
3
MARY ST
DIVISION ST
SCHOOL ST
TOURO ST
KAY ST
HIGH ST
9
6
5
CHURCH ST
CATHERINE
BELLEVUE AVE
4
AMERICA'S CUP AVE
MILL ST
REDWOO
8
MILL ST
7
OLD BEAC
PELHAM ST
MEMORIAL BLVD W

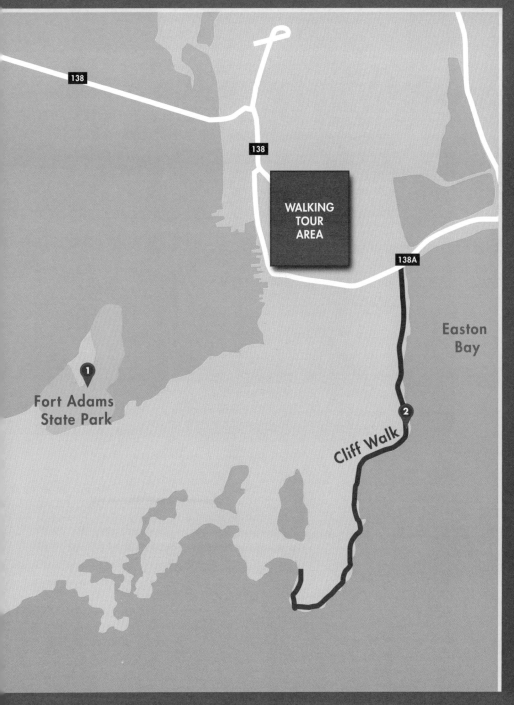

138

138

138A

WALKING TOUR AREA

Easton Bay

1 Fort Adams State Park

2 Cliff Walk

Newport Walking Tour Map

Other Sights in the Newport Area

Jamestown: The Lost City of Norumbega (?)

Jamestown docks. The epicenter of the town.

Just across Narragansett Bay from Newport, its more affluent and famous neighbor Jamestown seems to be frequently overlooked. That may be a good thing for people looking for the quintessential New England village with a town council, volunteer fire department, and harbor master watching the comings and goings of the yachts and boats at the pier. The tales of numerous hauntings, shipwrecks, and a demon dog from Hell chasing people for over three centuries only seems to add to the town's charm. The surrounding light houses and a windmill round out the quaint New England town feel that seems to be disappearing as more towns opt for chain stores and restaurants to replace acres of farmland and forested trails.

Like most small towns, the center is where most people begin a visit and most of the attractions are a mile or more away, but well worth a visit nonetheless. While the places of interest could be reached on foot, a bike or car may be a better mode of transportation than a sturdy pair of boots. The stretches of road with gentle hills and scent of the bay are more fitting for bicycles as opposed to the confines of a car with recycled air filtered to Freon levels of crispness. Regardless of how a person chooses to get around Conanicut Island, where Jamestown is located, they should expect the tour to be broken up into segments. The town was not designed with a tourist season in mind, but that is part of its charm. It invites people to wander off the trails and roads and find things that have not been visited by uncountable gaggles of tourists before.

The Walking Tour

1 Jamestown Waterfront and Narragansett Avenue

Gull over the water.

The best way to approach the island of Conanicut is by ferry from Newport. Passengers can see the Claiborne Pell Bridge, also called the Newport Bridge, which has connected Jamestown to Newport since 1969. Prior to the bridge being built, visitors relied on a more frequent ferry service that connected the two towns and dropped off passengers near the same spot they disembark at today.

Numerous piers and various types of boats can be viewed tied up at the docks, from commercial fishing craft to family yachts to smaller boats designed for a few passengers and a day at the most on the water. The days of car-carrying ferries is in Jamestown's past, and the bridges connecting the island to the eastern and

Bay View. The hotel that stood on this site was eventually replaced with the present day condominium complex, which kept some of the original's design queues.

Traps on the docks. Commercial fishing boats can be seen tied up alongside multi-million-dollar yachts in the summer.

western portions of Rhode Island mean the larger ferries are gone for good, leaving the harbor to the smaller water craft. The strong connection that Jamestown has always had with Narragansett Bay is still present today. What is missing are the abundance of inns that once welcomed people off the ferry.

Jamestown is still a summer community, but most of the community now resides in family homes or rental properties scattered around the island. Up until the 1970s, several inns and hotels dotted the waterfront and welcomed the spillover guests who couldn't find accommodation in Newport or were looking for a quieter place to stay. One throwback to those days still sits on the corner of Narragansett and Conanicus Avenues. The tower of Bay View condominium complex was fashioned after an old inn, Bay View Hotel, that once stood on the same corner and welcomed overnight guests to the small island. Overnight visitors are still welcomed today, but the inns are smaller and more scattered because the overnight guests have become fewer and fewer. Ironically, the bridge that made it easier to visit the island also made it easier for tourists to leave and stay at less expensive hotels on the mainland and making Jamestown an attraction for day visitors who appear to have become less frequent over the decades since the Pell Bridge has made it so easy to drive over the island in favor of better known attractions in western or eastern Rhode Island.

While the grand hotels that once graced the waterfront may be gone, other old-fashioned New England sites have remained and can be reached by walking up Narragansett Avenue, to the left of the Bay View condominium complex.

Before any trek is taken, visitors may want to fuel up on food and drinks. While there are numerous establishments offering food, ranging from light snacks to full course meals, one spot stands out for the numerous awards it has won for its entertainment as well as its eclectic mix of clientele.

2 Narragansett Café
25 Narragansett Avenue

At 25 Narragansett Avenue and boasting that they are open 365 days a year, "The Ganny" has been serving food and drink for decades and has been named best blues bar, neighborhood hangout, and best place for live music by *Rhode Island Monthly* numerous times. There may not be a bronze plaque announcing when they first opened their door, but *Rhode Island Monthly's* proclamations are prominently displayed for all diners and drinkers to view.

The focal U-shaped bar and rack behind it have seen better days, but that is part of the charm. No plastic or metal shelves adorned with mirrors but good old-fashioned woodwork that wears its chips and scrapes proudly and whispers of decades of rough clientele and the caring staff that did their best to smooth things over. A shuffleboard table on one side holds warning signs to new guests that it is a game table and not for setting drinks on. The only ATM has been shoved nearly out of sight in one corner, and the large screen TVs look like afterthoughts added to a bar designed for drinking and chatting in late afternoon after work has been finished for the day. "The Ganny" is a refreshing place when compared to the chain bars and restaurants that lure tourists in with promises of the same menu they can get at any of their other hundreds of locations.

Sea charts and pictures of ships from decades ago are on the walls, along with the before mentioned magazine awards, displayed alongside a few alcohol advertisements. The bar seems to have slowly come to terms with the eclectic clientele that has been setting foot in the wood- and stone-floored bar on a regular basis. One can imagine that it started off as a neighborhood hangout, then progressed when the first tourists pulled in to the dock down the street and found the cool, dark interior. The first game of pool between a mechanic in his oil-stained jeans and T-shirt against a Sperry-shoed, polo shirt-wearing boat owner must have been a sight as they kept score on the chalkboard that still stands over the pool table today.

The drink list seems to have adapted to the change in guests as well. It's hard to imagine the first drink served in the bar being a pinot noir, but the wine is served alongside all of its vineyard-raised cousins today, along with the more expected choice of beers, whiskies, and tequilas. It's not unusual to see a bottle of beer next to a boilermaker sitting alongside a chardonnay and all of the consumers deep in conversation. Snobbery and bias appear to be checked at the door—if any of the drinkers had it to begin with.

The one thing that appears to have not adapted to the change in clientele is the food menu. A solid selection of burgers and soups are the dominant selections in the bar, followed by the appetizers, all of which are great choices before venturing out on the paths of Jamestown. The New England standards of clam chowder and stuffed clams are, of course, on offer and are a good choice if a person is looking for a lighter fare.

The selection of drinks runs from an impressive wine list to whiskey and beer, but the Narragansett Café is better known for its selection of live music on weekends. Usually starting around nine p.m., the bar has become a destination for lovers of the blues as well as people searching for some of the best local bands and performers. The before mentioned awards speak volumes of the quality of the music offered at the bar.

Visitor Information

Menu and musical offerings are proudly displayed at www.narragansettcafe.com. Proclaiming that they are open 365 days a year and never charge a cover, "The Ganny" also proclaims their numerous awards from *Yankee Magazine* and *Rhode Island Monthly* for musical entertainment.

After having your fill of good food and drink, head west on Narragansett Avenue and cross the street to see if the Fire House Memorial is open.

3 Jamestown Fire Station and Fire Museum
50 Narragansett Avenue

At 50 Narragansett Avenue, the Jamestown Fire Station crew quite frequently can be seen tending to their gear and equipment in their expansive driveway and parking lot. From checking hoses to inspecting one of their inflatable boats, the volunteer fire department that services the island appears to be just as professional and well-equipped as any of the neighboring fire departments with full-time, salaried staff. During the summer months, the smaller, older fire house on the same lot is opened to the public as a memorial and museum, while it's larger, more modern neighbor is charged with watching over the community.

The main showpieces in the museum are the retired fire trucks and cart that once helped extinguish fires on the island.

Jamestown Fire Station. Some of the original horse drawn carriages are still in the old firehouse, which sits next to its modern replacement next door.

The oldest one is an 1894 Lafrance Steamer apparatus that was horse drawn over the hills and down the roads of Conanicut Island in the late nineteenth and early twentieth centuries. The polished steam chamber used to produce pressure for the hoses and analog gauges are well kept and demonstrate how much has changed in the century-plus when compared to one of its diesel powered, digitally read cousins next door. Two other retired engines in the museum exhibit the changes in automotive technology as well as firefighting techniques over the decades.

Roll-top desks and rotary phones decorate the office space where watchmen could be found twenty-four hours a day ready to answer any calls for assistance. The numerous photos of fires and flaming structures show that, while the island is quaint and residents relaxed, the job of firefighting is dangerous regardless of the community.

Visitor Information

The history of the Jamestown Fire Department is offered on www.jamestownfd.com. The museum is open during the summer, which is a great time to visit Rhode Island.

Exiting the fire house, continue west on Narragansett Avenue past the small churches and town hall, which exhibits the first land contract dividing up the island amongst colonists, and take a right onto North Main Road for a visit to the library and one particular item that may be proof of who arrived first, the Vikings or the British. The library's name is also non-tangible proof of some people's love of making stuff up.

4 Jamestown Philomenian Library

26 North Road

Back in 1828, according to the library's website, jamestownphilomenianlibrary.org, the Philomenian Debating Society finally agreed on the need for a library to service the island community, and each member graciously donated one dollar to the newly established book fund. The books were easier to come by than a permanent storage facility, which resulted in the first collection being scattered amongst the debating society member's homes, leaving one to imagine arguments about who would store the more scandalous titles and images. Town Hall and an old school house were also some of the homes for the collection up until 1971 when the permanent red-brick building was finally built.

In 1874, the debating society put up a convincing argument that another lending library on the island should join them in providing books to the community. The Jamestown Philomenian Library was born as well as a subtle joke. A place of learning and culture usually abhors fiction passed off as knowledge and fabricated factoids

87

are often shunned once discovered to be untrue, but the library seems to have embraced the made-up term "philomenian" and to this day still uses it in correspondence and titles.

"This is a coined word," the library's website so eloquently phrases it. "Philo" is Greek for love of but there is no root for "menian" and the library puts the word down to members of the debating club just making it up. Why is not explained. Perhaps it goes to the root of arguing. If a person figuratively throws a big word at someone, would the victim of the onslaught be willing to admit ignorance of the term? Some people won't and a smug feeling of superiority and cunning may be felt by the person making up the terms. Or maybe the user of the term honestly thought it was a word or was trying to add one to the English lexicon, similar to submissions to Urban Dictionary today. Regardless, it is one peculiarity of the island's past that the library has embraced and visitors can brag of visiting the one and only Philomenian library anywhere in the world.

Visitors can also see some items in the Sydney L. Wright Museum, which occupies a room on the premises that has left a few people scratching their heads. The museum houses a collection of items from the West Ferry archeological site, which was first discovered in 1936 and properly excavated in 1966 and '67. Many of the items have been attributed to the Narragansett and other local tribes as well as colonists with a theory that Conanicut Island served as a middle ground for trade between the western part of modern-day Rhode Island and the eastern shores of the state as well as Massachusetts, which it borders.

Amongst the clay pipe that likely originated in England and whetstones used for sharpening fish hooks and knives are brass plates that stand out because of their shape and possible origin. "They were probably used for breast ornaments, or as a crude form of armor," the exhibit description states. It goes on to compare the plates to similar pieces of brass that were found on a skeleton in Fall River, Massachusetts, in 1832, about fifteen miles up the bay from the island. "The Skeleton in Armor," as the Fall River discovery became known as, led to numerous theories about Viking voyages to the area as far back as the tenth century because of the design of the armor as well as the calculated age of the remains. While the exhibit describes the theories as "tenuous," there is some evidence backing up the traveling Norsemen theory as well as a possibility that Narragansett Bay may have been the home of the lost city of Norumbega.

As far back as the early 1500s, European mapmakers and explorers attributed the name Norumbega to spots all over present-day New England. It was believed that Vikings had made the journey across the Atlantic well before the European fleets and possibly set up their own colonies in the wilds of the North American continent. According to Eben Norton Horsford in his 1891 book *Defences of Norumbega,* numerous maps existed that gave the general location of the lost Viking city in the vicinity of New England and some oddities, such as mysterious stone towers and rocks with cryptic imagery and writing, in the area were used to back up this claim.

Horsford placed the Viking colony farther north in Massachusetts, but the entrance to Norumbega from the sea was supposed to be wide with a stretch of land dividing the waterway in half, similar to Conanicut Island in Narragansett Bay. There were raging rapids farther up the waterway, similar to the now concrete covered Quequechan River in Fall River, where the Skeleton in Armor was found. Dighton Rock with its possible Norse runes was also found along the shores of the Taunton River just north of Fall River. Looking east from one stubby peninsula on Conanicut a person would possibly see a light from the famed Newport Tower which may have been built by the Viking colonists as a lookout post.

Combined with the different burial practices found on the West Ferry Site—some people were simply interred while others were cremated—there is a "tenuous" argument for the possibility that Narragansett Bay at least was once the home of Vikings as well as possibly one of the sites for the lost city of Norumbega. The geography of present-day Jamestown makes it an ideal spot for a colony as well. From high points on the island, people can watch for approaching groups traveling by boat. Conanicut is large enough to farm and breed livestock on and timber is still abundant today, so crafting a home or ship 1,000 years ago would have simply required skilled labor because the raw materials were already there.

Are the brass plates in the Sydney L. Wright Museum all that remain of a Viking community that found the geography and access to the ocean from Conanicut Island ideal for travel and trade? Were the last members of the Norse community cremated and their ashes buried alongside the bodies of the Narragansett on the West Ferry Site? Possible, but it is unlikely that anyone will ever know for certain. The dots are there but connecting them into a coherent image and definitive answer is difficult, if not impossible.

Lack of concrete evidence has contributed to the myth and legend of Vikings walking the stony shores of New England and pushing long boats out into the bay. What is still visible today is the remnants of the US Navy and US Army who were charged with defending the bay from invading forces from the American Revolution up until the late twentieth century. While there is still a strong navy presence in the Newport and Jamestown area, their forces have been reduced, but the forts they once occupied can still be visited, like the navy ammunition bunkers on Prudence Island or Fort Adams in Newport.

The southern tip of Jamestown has been the home of fortifications since the American Revolution, and if some tales are to be believed, it is still the home of a demon dog that has chased numerous people over the centuries right up to today, and the present structure, Fort Wetherill, is still home to seafaring parties but of more commercial and recreational parties.

Visitor Information

The small library and museum has perhaps one of the longest web addresses (www. jamestownphilomenianlibrary.org) where the history of their unique name is explained alongside information about events and their collections.

Other Sights in the Jamestown Area

1 Fort Wetherill

3 Fort Wetherill Road

Fort Wetherill. Graffiti makes for poor camouflage.

Roughly a mile south of the center of Jamestown, down Walcott Avenue, Fort Wetherill presently hosts everything from SCUBA diving groups walking into the ocean from one of the coves to commercial fishing boats that tie up near the old mine storage facilities that have been turned into small museums with scant descriptions of what the waterfront looked like up to the 1950s. Judging solely on a graffiti scale, the most popular parts of the park are the old gun emplacements, which once guarded the passageway leading to Providence.

The twelve- and six-inch guns that faced the water are long gone and the projectile of choice appears to be aerosol paint, which seems to cover every square inch of the concrete and steel that is still there today and likely will be there for decades to come. The fortress was built to withstand the onslaught of naval artillery and trying to remove it with civilian tools appears to be impossible, so the town has left it to continue to silently watch over the bay. Some attempts have been made to clean it up, including a work crew from a prison who painted the entire structure gray one summer, according to a resident, but the gray was quickly covered with a multitude of neon and other shades again.

Other forms of vandalism include the removal of doors and obstructions so people could gain access to the long, unlit tunnels that run the length of the fort. Despite suggestions not to enter, people still can be seen exiting the doorways with extinguished flashlights in hand. Some of those visitors have decorated the interior with paint as well, but some have come for another, less artistic, more macabre, reason. Quite a few have come searching for ghosts and in particular the Black Dog of Fort Wetherill.

"The Phantom Dog of Fort Wetherill" is the November 17, 2014, headline from the *Yankee Xpress* that describes the beast that is alleged to have scared everyone from the British when they first set foot on the land in the 1770s up to modern times. "Witnesses have seen the wraith approaching them with its glowing red eyes and white fangs protruding from its gaping mouth," Thomas D'Agostino wrote in the article. Other manifestations include barking being heard throughout the tunnels and visions of the dog walking through walls and doors.

A visit by another writer, Lauren Neslusan, found graffiti related to "…Satanic rituals…," which she described in her March 24, 2010, Examiner.com article "The dark tunnels of Fort Wetherill." She also described "…uneasy.." feelings and the passages as "…the perfect claustrophobic nightmare." Neither D'Agostino or Neslusan

reported any personal interaction with the dog themselves, but the tale has been told for centuries resulting in a little-reported local legend.

It is perhaps why the area is a popular stop for self-described ghost hunters who have visited the fort and posted their findings to YouTube and other online sites. The history of the fort includes falling to the British in the American Revolution, then being taken over by American troops who maintained a presence there watching the entrance to one of the most important shipping channels on the East Coast, right up until the land was given to the State of Rhode Island in 1972. This history may contribute to the ominous feelings some people get when they visit.

During World War II, the fort was used as a prisoner of war camp, and the SCUBA clubs that have made the area a popular spot for diving may be swimming over one of the numerous wrecks that have found the seventy-foot cliffs and rocky beaches the cause of an abrupt end

Tunnels of Fort Wetherill. Unlit and with the floor missing in places, entering the tunnels is not advised. The wandering Hound from Hell is another deterrent to consider.

to the long journeys they took. Some of the wrecks may be the intentional ones the British sunk as a way to close off portions of the area to French and American vessels during the 1770s. The southern end of the island appears to be a magnet for bad luck and superstitions.

One less famous apparition may be making the rounds nearby, and one can easily imagine seeing "The Gray Lady," as she is known, wandering over to the fort from her home, Wetherledge.

Atop the hill that overlooks the graffiti-covered fort, Wetherledge is a "cottage" built in 1889, according to the home's website Wetherledge.com, by the mysterious Ms. Rice from Worcester, Massachusetts. What makes Ms. Rice an enigma is that no one seems to know her first name, and there are no images of her to be found. She appears to have arrived one day, purchased the land, built her house looking out over Narragansett Bay, and lived there in peace. The present owner believes Ms. Rice is still there.

"She doesn't really do anything to me," Ms. Jane Scott present owner and resident of Wetherledge says of The Gray Lady who has been seen walking the grounds in the early evening. Ms. Scott has lived on the private estate since the '80s when she first bought it after getting lost on her way to Newport. The home, which used to be the officer's club for Fort Wetherill when the navy was stationed there, still projects elegance with fine woodwork, well-stocked library, and spacious porch with fireplace looking out over the field towards the fort and beyond into the bay. One can see why the previous owner, if the ghost is indeed Ms. Rice, may not want to leave and one can imagine that she may enjoy the weddings that the estate hosts.

Ms. Scott doesn't have any tales of the Black Dog of Fort Wetherill, but she has a few concerning The Gray Lady and her likes and dislikes. "Patrick the boat captain woke up one night getting a back rub." Patrick, who had rented one of the rooms on the estate while his ship was in port, appeared to be upset by the phantasmal masseuse and took off the next day leaving some of his belongings behind. The Gray Lady has not always been so caressing of visitors.

Ms. Scott said that a person who used to rent the house before she bought it was walking through the rooms to make sure that everything had been packed before driving off. "He walked in front of the dart board...," and an old fashioned dart embedded itself in the board he had just passed. Ms. Scott theorizes that The Gray Lady may not have liked the idea that the renter intended to become the owner of the property. "She wanted me here."

Ms. Scott also believes the ghost may "...flip out..." if she intended to sell the house and move out, but that doesn't seem to concern her. "She likes being here." And so does Ms. Scott, adding that, "I may come back to haunt it"—perhaps leading to a third spirit wandering the Fort Wetherill area in the future. Chatting with Ms. Jane Scott for a few minutes will convince just about anyone that she would be a pleasant ghost who perhaps would be seen in deep conversation with The Gray Lady as they stroll across the grounds.

After Fort Wetherill, a visit to one of the oldest lighthouses in the country is recommended: Beavertail.

Visitor Information

History of the former navy officer's club as well as contact information for people looking to have a wedding or place to stay can be found at www.wetherledge.com. Pictures of the apartments are also on display.

2 Beavertail Lighthouse and Park

Beavertail State Park, Beavertail Road

Beavertail and the keeper's house. Now lit by electricity, the original oil lit lamp guided ships around the outcroppings of rock that have plagued the waterways for centuries.

Heading back towards downtown Jamestown, turn left going westwards onto Hamilton Avenue and continue until it intersects with Southwest Avenue, then over the narrow isthmus that connects the far southwest side of the island with its larger eastern neighbor.

Heading across, visitors can see the large farmland, dotted with stone walls that made the island an ideal spot for farming. The lush grass and dense woods were perfect for constructing farms and homes and tending to the livestock that could support the community and be sold to markets in the other parts of the state. Of course the days before the bridges connected the island to the mainland, east and west of the island, boats and ferries were the primary modes of transportation for getting the produce to market off the island. Shipping is not without its dangers and the Beavertail Lighthouse, at the end of Beavertail Road was one of the many

Beavertail Lighthouse. One of the more majestic lighthouses in Rhode Island.

lighthouses in the area constructed to assist in navigating the rocky passageways of Narragansett Bay.

Atop the rocky cliffs, facing south, the granite tower and white house to the side have been assisting boats since the mid-nineteenth century, but history of lighthouses and navigational aids on the site go farther back to the American Revolution when colonists erected a wooden tower on the tip of Beavertail, so named because it resembles the tail of the aquatic mammal. British troops took over the area in the 1770s and, when they withdrew, burned the structure but not before taking the vital components of the light with them, according to lighthousefriends.com.

The unique location led to many structures having to be rebuilt over the centuries because of the proximity to the water finally culminating in the present structure, which still helps in navigation but is more a tourist draw for the land-dwelling residents. A pair of air horns protruding from the house next to the tower remind visitors that lighthouses were not solely a visual aid but auditory as well.

From the front of the lighthouse, Block Island can be frequently seen on the distant horizon, roughly twelve miles from the rocky shores. In the western passage, an outcropping of rock resembles a surfaced submarine which, according to some of the plaques in the park, led to scares during the world wars, as residents reported German submarines rising from the depths. The tip of the island is also one of the few spots on Conanicut where people can see both sides of Rhode Island: the more urbanized east side as well as the far more rural western portion of the state.

Today, visitors may be more concerned about the brisk breeze than submarines surfacing or ships getting dangerously close to the shore, and the protection they would likely be needing are jackets and hats as the area has turned into a park. It seems that there are always visitors on the grounds, regardless of the time of year, taking in the views and enjoying the sea air. While the main lighthouse and museum, which is open from mid-June to September, are the main buildings on site, there are a few other structures which can be found.

One structure is an old observation post facing east whose entrance has been blocked up by stones. Some enthusiastic visitors over the decades have dug out enough space for people to crawl in and see the concrete tunnels the navy and army built as a command structure for the coastal artillery, which watched over the bay but never fired a shot in anger. Entering the tunnels is not suggested, but some people still scamper into the tunnels nonetheless.

More people seem to enjoy traversing the rocks looking out over the water, and some adventurous souls have even gone as far as setting up portable BBQ sets and picnicking on the hard stones and boulders. What they lack in comfort they certainly make up in views as the crashing waves and passing water craft make for a relaxing backdrop to long days and weeks.

If you have taken the foresight to pack a lunch and a few drinks, the grass is a fine place to settle and end the day. Caution should be had if you choose to venture out onto the rocks: picnic in peace and away from precarious cliffs and tunnels.

Jamestown has centuries of history that is frequently dwarfed by its neighbor Newport but a trip to the other City by the Sea would likely be a pleasant one as long as you don't mind risking the wrath of a demon dog or heated arguments about who came first the Vikings or the British.

Visitor Information

Beavertail Lighthouse is on the grounds of one of Rhode Island's most majestic state parks. Maps and history of the lighthouse, which became a military base later to become a park, can be found at www.riparks.com.

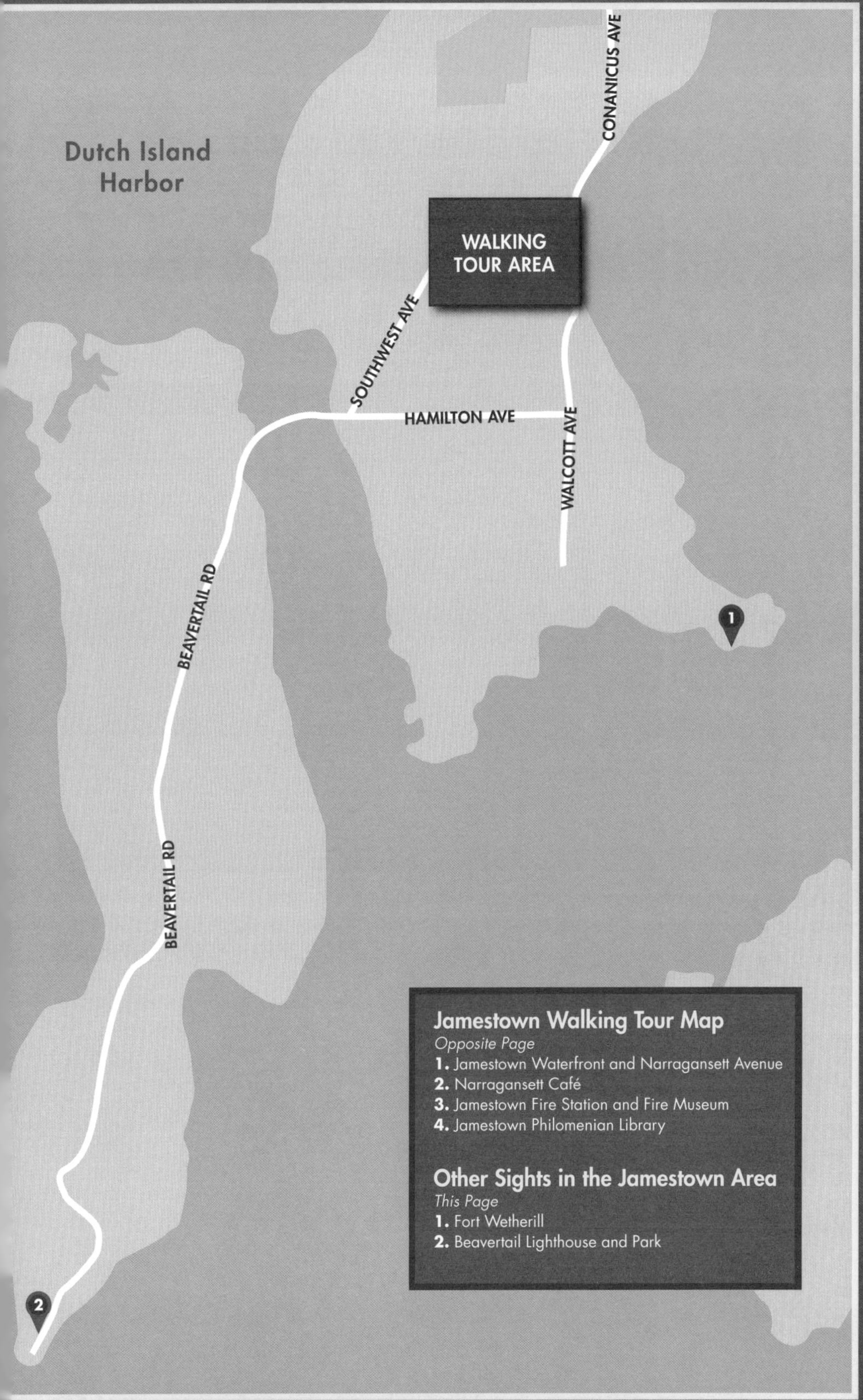

Dutch Island
Harbor

CONANICUS AVE

WALKING
TOUR AREA

SOUTHWEST AVE

HAMILTON AVE

WALCOTT AVE

BEAVERTAIL RD

BEAVERTAIL RD

1

2

Jamestown Walking Tour Map
Opposite Page
1. Jamestown Waterfront and Narragansett Avenue
2. Narragansett Café
3. Jamestown Fire Station and Fire Museum
4. Jamestown Philomenian Library

Other Sights in the Jamestown Area
This Page
1. Fort Wetherill
2. Beavertail Lighthouse and Park

Cookie-Baking Ghosts, Colonial Commandos, and Other Oddities in the Ocean State

Waves on the rocks. Some of the perils to navigating New England waters.

Sadly, not all places of interest line up within walking distance of other sites people may enjoy visiting. "Off the beaten path" can occasionally have a near literal meaning. Some "off the map" sites are interesting for the history, others for mere natural wonder, and a few are even able to combine both. Other destinations are worth visiting for the supernatural tales associated with them. Tales of alleged giants within walking distance of ghostly monks, spectral wanderers on rough paths, cookie-baking spirits and the location where one of the unluckiest generals of the American Revolution was kidnapped for the second time are just some of the spots in Rhode Island often overlooked but certainly worth a visit.

Most of the following sites can be enjoyed as day trips and enthusiastic travelers may even be able to cram two or more of the sites into a one-day itinerary. Regardless, the following spots are a nice journey away from crowds and cities for the most part.

Four Sights to See

1 Fort Barton

340–360 Highland Road, Triverton

Listed as one of Rhode Island's "Challenging Hikes" by *Hey Rhody*, a magazine dedicated to outdoor travel and interests, Fort Barton in Tiverton is approximately three miles of trails crisscrossing over swamps and through dark woods. The "fort" in the park's name comes from the fact that the high ground that it occupies was used as a gun emplacement during the American Revolution when colonists built earthen walls and fired onto Aquidneck Island and ships in the bay. During the war, the British occupied Aquidneck and colonists would take pot shots and organize raids from the Tiverton side. The British, naturally, would take offense and fire back. The quiet woods and quaint view is a far cry from the days of amphibious attacks and artillery exchanges that the area was once notorious for.

The earthen mounds are still there today and an open-topped tower offers visitors a view over the bay to the island that was on the receiving end of the cannon balls lobbed from the "fort" below. A small cemetery north of the tower is an old family plot that is marked on maps that can be picked up at the Town Hall, which is literally across the street from the park's entrance at 99 Lawton Avenue. Maps and sturdy footwear are strongly recommended for the hike into the woods, which have a longer and bloodier history than a group of disagreeing colonists. Along with the usual dangers of broken trail, low-hanging trees, swamps, and deer ticks, some people believe a supernatural risk resides in the woods.

According to Elon Cook in an article he wrote for Sakonnethistorical.org, "Sin and Flesh Brook," the spirit of Zoeth Howland may occasionally be seen along the trails and waterways where his life was brutally ended. On March 28, 1676, Howland was making his way to a Quaker service from his home in Dartmouth, Massachusetts, to Newport, which had the closest Quaker meeting house. As he approached the shores, where he was likely going to catch a ferry to Aquidneck to continue his pilgrimage, he was approached by a party of Native Americans. The last journey of Zoeth Howland was in the second year of King Phillip's War.

The Wampanoag, Narragansett, and Nipmuck tribes formed an alliance in 1675 and waged a campaign of guerilla fighting against the colonists who were overrunning the land and forcing the tribes onto smaller and smaller plots. The campaign became known as King Phillip's War, named after the title and name that the English gave to the Wampanoag leader Metacom. Some accounts of the war stated that it was the bloodiest campaign fought in New England and resulted in numerous towns being torched, farms destroyed and thousands of lives lost—Zoeth Howland being one of them.

The group that he came across tortured him and tossed his body into a nearby stream. Howland's body was found later and the nameless stream became known as "Sinning Flesh Brook," according to Cook's article. One of the attackers, Manasses or Molasses (depending on which source is being referenced), was convicted of the murder and sold into slavery like many of the Native Americans who fought against the colonists. The war itself ended in 1678 when the last leader of the Native Americans, Metacom, was killed and his dismembered body passed off to the colonists. Metacom's head was carried to Plymouth where it was placed for all to see.

Today some people have allegedly seen a spirit wandering the trails where Howland, a peaceful Quaker, was murdered. Is his restless spirit wandering the trails seeking revenge? Unlikely, considering the pious and peaceful reputation of the Quakers. Perhaps he is wandering in confusion, feeling the need to warn other travelers of dangers along the trail? Is it possible that the apparition that has been seen along the course of Sin and Flesh Brook, as it is known today, is upset that the wrong man was convicted and sold into a life of servitude for a crime he didn't commit? There is also a chance that the right man was convicted but the forgiving nature of Howland is upset that a man was so severely punished.

If you happen to wander across Mr. Howland in your trek through the woods past the marshy Sin and Flesh Brook that snakes through Fort Barton, feel free to ask.

The park is open from sunrise to sunset and a small mailbox, near the paved roadway that leads up to the tower and entrance to the trails, frequently has copies of maps. Maps in a PDF format can also be downloaded from www.tiverton.ri.gov on their attractions page. The longest trail is about three miles in length but there are a few trails to hike, which may make a trip slightly longer than anticipated. If you plan to make a day of it, bring a lunch and something to drink. There are a few restaurants and convenience stores within driving and biking distance, but wandering into a haunted forest without the bare essentials has all the making of a horror movie, and a forest with a stream called Sin and Flesh is scary enough.

2 Prescott Farm

2009 West Main Road, Middletown

Most people think of Rhode Island's neighbor Massachusetts as having the best tales to tell of the American Revolution, Boston Tea Party, Bunker Hill, and Paul Revere riding through the streets warning people of a pre-Beatles British invasion. Rhode Islanders are proud of the *Gaspee* affair where a revenue ship was unfortunate enough to get stuck in a sand bar and was torched by irate smugglers and shop owners. A lesser-known event took place in Rhode Island and had a greater influence on the American Revolution than the torching of a ship: the kidnapping of a general.

General Richard Prescott was the commander in charge of British troops during the occupation of Newport, located on the southern end of Aquidneck Island. While the town of Newport was being looted and shopkeepers and residents not loyal to the British were fleeing, General Prescott gained a notorious reputation of locking

Windmill at Prescott Farm. Once the scene of a dramatic kidnapping, the windmill and trails are more welcoming today.

up captured revolutionaries on any of the numerous prison ships that littered Newport harbor and Narragansett Bay, frequently indefinitely. The conditions on the ships led to countless deaths, and disease was easily spread through the cramped quarters. It is likely the constant reminders of the death in the harbor led Gen. Prescott to seek fresher air farther north on the island at the home of Henry J. Overing, a loyalist and owner of Overing Farm.

While the eastern side of the island was being riddled with cannon shot and subjected to raids from the colonists in Tiverton, across the water, the western side of the island where the Overing family resided was deemed safe. British warships and a greater distance from the western shores of Rhode Island gave the illusion of protection. That illusion was shattered by William Barton, colonial revolutionary and the person that Fort Barton was named after.

According to the exceptionally informative Newport Restoration Foundation website about the history of Prescott Farm, a mercenary general named Charles Lee was captured and deemed vital to the American fighting plans. General George Washington needed a prisoner of equal rank to exchange for Lee, and William Barton had his eyes on Prescott and a plan was formed.

Kidnapping the Enemy: The Special Operations to Capture General Charles Lee and Richard Prescott by Christian McBurney details how Barton guided several boats from the west coast of Rhode Island, past Prudence Island in the bay, avoided British warships, and beached on the western coast of Aquidneck Island on July 10, 1777. Barton interviewed several deserters while planning the raid, according to the book, and knew that General Prescott frequently made overnight trips to the farm from Newport with a small number of troops as bodyguards. Racing across the fields, Barton challenged the guard outside Prescott's quarters and entered the house. Prescott must have been familiar with the routine since this was the second time that he had been captured by colonial troops, the first time in Quebec a couple of years earlier.

Today, it is easier to approach Prescott Farm, which had been renamed to reflect the unfortunate general, and park in the modest parking lot at 2009 West Main Road, Portsmouth. The windmill that is close to the lot overlooks the fields and

A small bridge on Prescott Farm that has been troll free since 1978.

buildings on the estate and is one of the many parks and structures in the state that have been saved/preserved by Doris Duke and the Newport Restoration Foundation that she helped fund. Today, instead of a fast food restaurant or gas station, visitors can view a working farm that reflects what colonists and farmers had to deal with as they toiled on the land to survive.

The small red house that was the target for the audacious Barton raid still stands a short distance from the windmill and near the herb garden. Other attractions on the farm include the prominent windmill, a "recent" addition from the early 1800s, according to the Newport Restoration Foundation, as well as older houses and residences, some of which are privately rented and not open to the public. Short hiking trails and fields are the finishing touches to the grounds. Occasionally there is a welcoming committee of geese roaming the parking lot and trails—who can become a bit aggressive at times.

Prescott Farm is not off the beaten path by any stretch of the imagination; in fact, a paved highway is mere feet from the entrance. This is a case where the convenience of paved roads and high speed limits has led to one of the state's gems being overlooked for the crown jewels of the Newport mansions farther along the road, which thousands of people speed to annually. The grounds could be covered in a morning or afternoon and is well worth a stop for the history as well as the view. Please remember that kidnapping is frowned upon by the staff and residents there today.

Visitor Information

Prescott Farm and the surrounding trails come under the jurisdiction of the Newport Restoration Foundation. Their web page (www.newportrestoration.org) offers information about the farm as well as other locations they have been helping to preserve.

3 Rose Island Lighthouse

Rose Island Lighthouse. A throwback to the days when ships were guided by map reading and manual plotting, not GPS and computer.

Ferry service from Newport and Jamestown is available for day trips to one of the oldest functioning lighthouses in the country, and like any good maritime structure or attraction in Rhode Island, the staff is friendly and the ghosts keep mostly to themselves, except when they're baking cookies.

The lighthouse has faced the usual dangers of foul weather, precariously guided vessels, and budget cuts, but the lighthouse was once abandoned and had to deal with scavengers who would strike out to the island in search of scrap that could be sold for a profit on the mainland. One imagines brass fixings and copper wiring were the goals for such trips to the lighthouse and Fort Hamilton, which also inhabits the island, and little was done to curtail the destruction to the buildings for quite some time.

In 1984, according to roseislandlighthouse.org, volunteers from Newport went out to the island and started to do something about the dire conditions of the lighthouse, which had become a rust- and graffiti-covered eye sore in the bay, and began the process of restoring it to what it looked like in 1912. On August 7, 1993, the restorations were completed and the light was once again lit, making the island a private aid to navigation.

According to lighthousefriends.com, the lighthouse, which is close to land, was considered one of the better postings a lighthouse keeper could hope for in the United States Lighthouse Service, which eventually merged with the United States Coast Guard in 1939, but the weather took its toll on the building and the staff. Winds shifted the tower so much that plaster had cracked on the interior in 1876; it was flooded in November of the same year, and the winter's supply of vegetables were ruined. The harsh weather, which seems to take a greater toll on the island than the mainland, may be why the building of Fort Hamilton on the northern side of the island was abandoned in 1800. A round wall can still be seen today, which is the remains of the oldest fortification on the island. All of the dangers didn't keep the US Navy from using the island as storage for torpedoes during the world wars though, in the long brick and mortar building not far from the lighthouse.

One of the more interesting tales about the lighthouse keepers is Jesse Orton, keeper from 1921 to 1936, who bought a cow on the mainland and had it transported to the island on the Jamestown ferry. No mention is made of how the cow got on the ferry but its exit was certainly talked about for years. According to lighthousefriends. com, the ferry captain pulled up to the shore of the island and tried to lower a gangplank for the cow to walk on. The crew gave up and lowered the cow by cable into the surf, and with shouts of encouragement from bystanders, the cow began the arduous swim to shore. With frightened moos drowned out by crashing waves, the bovine made it to the beach and collapsed. It stayed there for a day and then summoned enough strength to be guided to the pen where Orton used it for milk. Like other lighthouse keepers in the region he kept a small garden and pen for livestock near his house, much to the annoyance of the navy personnel charged with maintaining the storage facilities for torpedoes on the other side of the island, who occasionally had to explain property lines to cows and pigs.

Today, visitors are told about the property lines in an effort to protect birds that have found the island a perfect place to nest. Sea gulls and migratory birds dominate the lion's share of the island from April to mid-August as they build nests and raise their young far from the roads and congested streets of Newport and surrounding cities. Visitors are asked to respect the lines set up and not to venture past marked points in an effort to protect the young birds and to also protect the visitors. Sea gulls have a reputation of attacking people they see as possibly harmful to their young. The birds may be aggressive, but the ghost is of the friendly variety.

One of the more bizarre ghost tales in Rhode Island was written about by Jennifer Huget in an August 28, 2002, article for the *Washington Post*, which was reprinted on the roseislandlighthouse.org web page. Ms. Huget and her family took the Rose Island Lighthouse Foundation up on their offer to be keepers for a week, which is still an option visitors can look into, and mentions the spirit of Christina Curtis, the wife of the original lighthouse keeper who has taken it upon herself to bake sugar cookies into the wee hours of the morning for children and presumably the occasional adult not afraid of supernaturally prepared baked goods.

Visitor Information

The lighthouse has been open to tours during the summer months for years and is a popular destination for people hoping to escape the occasionally congested streets of Newport. Day trips are a good way to see the house and grounds, but leisurely adventurous overnight stays can be arranged at roseislandlighthouse.org as well as options to become a keeper for a week. In lieu of room service, people opting to stay overnight get a spectacular view and a chance at a sugar cookie baked by Christina Curtis.

The website www.roseislandlighthouse.org offers a detailed history of the building's construction, abandonment, and eventual rebirth. Information about staying at the lighthouse is also provided for those looking for a beautiful, secluded getaway

4 Cumberland Public Library

1464 Diamond Hill Road, Cumberland

Some folks visit for the books, others enjoy the trails out back, history buffs come to view the nation's oldest war memorial, and numerous people have an eye for the supernatural aspects of the Cumberland Public Library. To say that the present library grounds have catered to a wide variety of visitors over the centuries is an understatement.

At 1464 Diamond Hill Road, off a main street and surrounded mostly by woods, the library has become an epicenter of entertainment and meeting space for the community of Cumberland. The modern facility was tacked on to the remains of a monastery that occupied the grounds until it burned in 1950 and houses most of the library's collection. The granite monastery part of the structure is used primarily for meetings of local clubs and library sponsored organizations, like the chess club or anime appreciation society. The ghosts who are alleged to wander the halls and rooms of the library don't appear to be restricted to the older part of the building with some reports of books being removed from shelves during hours when the library is closed as well as shadowy figures being seen in front of the main entrance.

The second-story corridor still retains the original tiles and imagery of a cross embedded in the floor, reminding visitors of the more pious days of the building. Wide windows look out on to the entrance and the field where the Trappist monks, who once called the place home, buried their deceased and which has been turned into a small park where the more common sight is someone basking in the sun on warm days and not shrouded shades flittering around the stonework and trees. Copies of newspapers describing the 1950 fire that convinced the monks to abandon Cumberland, where they had been since 1900, are placed on the walls in the corridor and this is also near a recorded, alleged haunting.

On an episode of *Ghost Hunters*, which aired February 26, 2014, the library was the topic and the lady's room was the focus of a recorded event where the faucets

Cumberland Library. Former monastery, site of a massacre, and location to what could be the oldest war memorial in North America, the Cumberland Library is also rumored to be haunted.

would turn on and off without help from the living. Other reports from the same episode include sounds of books being leafed through in the second-floor reading room of the library, through the doors at the north end of the corridor. The same episode reports that the elevator occasionally goes straight to the third floor of the building, which is closed to the public and is where the monks would restrict their sick. Numerous deaths were reported on the third floor, and one can wonder if the spirits that are alleged to haunt the second floor are merely looking for a quieter place to haunt.

The macabre history of the library is not restricted to the building but radiates out over the 500 acres of the grounds. Several miles of hiking trails cover the old quartz quarry, which contributed to the name of Diamond Road, irrigation ponds, and wide, open fields and paths. Most of the trails have quaint names such as Whipple Loop or Monk's Quarry Trail and are recent additions, as in the last century or so, but one of the trails is also likely the oldest path still in use in northwestern Rhode Island. It also has the distinction of having the most unnerving name on the grounds: Nine Men's Misery Trail.

"The Nine Men's Misery monument is located in a quiet, dark, uninviting place in the woods…" When a web page dedicated to promoting tourism, visitrhodeisland. com, describes a spot as uninviting, you know it's bad. The cairn was erected by British soldiers in 1676 when they came across the remains of nine men who were captured and tortured by Native Americans during King Phillips War. At the top of a hill in the woods, near a stone wall today, the bodies were covered with rocks and the location memorialized as the troops continued tracking the killers through the woods. Over the centuries, the bodies had been dug up, reburied, and have been the subject of numerous stories about the woods and the strange things that have been reported there.

According to "A Haunting Attraction in Rhode Island" by Kathleen Burge and published on boston.com, December 5, 2007, the battle that saw the demise of the nine men began on March 26, 1676. They were with a larger group that was overrun by Narragansett fighters and the nine colonists broke north for what they believed to be safety. They were eventually captured and allegedly tortured on the hill where the marker is today.

The loose stones that covered the deceased were removed, according to the article, in the late 1700s by a group of men who may have been medical students. It appears to have always been a morbid destination for people and to prevent visitors from digging around the entombed the stones were eventually cemented in place—when no one seems to know. The plaque that describes the tale of the Nine Men's Misery was placed on the cairn in 1928 by the State of Rhode Island as a more permanent marker and description of the event that contributed to the name of the spot. The fact that the British soldiers who first came across the deceased in the seventeenth century erected the stones makes an argument for this being the oldest war memorial in the United States and possibly all of North America.

"For years, rumors have persisted that Nine Men's Misery is haunted. Some say they've seen a man on horseback; others report a monk or a child," Burge wrote. Perhaps the monk is a wayward spirit from the library, former monastery, out stretching his ghostly legs; the child could be a spirit of someone who once lived and played in the woods. The horseman could be anyone from the 1600s. But one unique thing stands out more than most to some people: the shadow that Benjamin Bucklin, one of the nine men interred there, cast over the site.

History Channel investigators Bill and Jim Vieira descended on the Nine Men's Misery Trail in search of giants. Their show *Search for the Lost Giants* chronicles their journeys around the world as they seek evidence of an alleged race of giants that some believe once populated spots around the globe. According to a *Valley Breeze* article published November 19, 2014, "Giants at Nine Men's Misery? History Channel Investigators on the Job" by Editor Marcia Green, Benjamin Bucklin was known as being a giant and having a peculiar set of "…two rows of teeth." According to the article, the remains of the nine men were re-interred on the site in 1976, after spending time in scattered family graves and in historical societies, and the Vieira brothers were in town hoping to speak with someone who may have seen the remains of Bucklin being buried again that day in '76 who may have noticed anything unusual, such as the reported extra set of teeth or abnormal height.

Regardless of whether a person stumbles across a ghost, gets a deal at the bookstore connected to the library, or spends a fine day wandering across the streams and over the hills of Cumberland, the library and the adjoining grounds have a lot to offer and makes for a fine destination. The secluded forests seem to have gained a reputation as an uninviting place, but that is far from the truth. Wide open paths, looping trails, and an abundance of maps available at the library or online at cumberlandlibrary.org help visitors find their way.

Visitor Information

The history of building as well as maps to the trails that break off into the woods can all be seen at www.cumberlandlibrary.org. Updates on special events are listed alongside the hours and listings of the services at the library. There are very few places in America that offer a notary public in the same place where the spirits of deceased monks are believed to stroll.

Cookie-Baking Ghosts, Colonial Commandos, and Other Oddities in the Ocean State: 4 Sights to See
1. Fort Barton
2. Prescott Farm
3. Rose Island Lighthouse
4. Cumberland Public Library

Conclusion

Rhode Island is better known for the mansions of Newport, the capital with its numerous colleges and universities, and, of course, H. P. Lovecraft, as well as the fine Italian restaurants of Federal Hill. Wandering off the usual routes taken by visitors can lead to lesser-known treasures that are more commonly the "haunts" of locals.

On a day when the tour buses are lining up outside one of the stone gate entrances to a Newport mansion, a trip to less-congested Jamestown may be rejuvenating. While the latest haunted tour of one of Rhode Island's cities may be nearly sold out and/or (*shudder*) congested with selfie -taking children, wandering off on your own with one of the enclosed tours may be a more peaceful option that promises a bit of historical ghost storytelling.

Grab some comfortable footwear, check the weather, and head out on your own or with some friends for a trip. If you get lost, you'll likely find your way again. If it starts to rain, pop in for a bite to eat or a relaxing beverage somewhere. Go at your own pace and enjoy the day, or night if you are more adventurous, and read one of the numerous tales of murder, death, and ghosts that the littlest state has to offer. The often overlooked tales are sometimes the most interesting.

I hope that I can be your guide through this collection!

Bibliography

Albanese, Ellen. "Doris Duke Foundation Reinvents Queen Anne Square." *Boston Globe*, May 25, 2013.

Beckwith, Henry L. "Lovecraft's Providence and Adjacent Places." Hampton Falls, NH: Donald M. Grant Inc. 1986.

Burge, Kathleen. "A Haunting Attraction in Rhode Island." Boston.com, December 5, 2007.

Canney, Donald L. "Rum War: The US Coast Guard and Prohibition." Coast Guard Bicentennial Series, 2006.

Case of Turk's Head vs. Broderick. www.leagle.com.

"Coast Guard Shoots Rumrunner." *New Bedford Evening Standard*, December 29, 1929.

Cook, Elan. "Sin and Flesh Brook." Sakonnethistorical.org.

Cusumano, Katherine. "The Truth Laid Bare: Naked Donut Run Sweetens Reading Period." *Brown Daily Herald*, January 23, 2013.

D'Agostino, Thomas. "The Phantom Dog of Fort Wetherill." *Yankee Express*, November 17, 2014.

Dix, John Ross. "A Handbook of Newport and Rhode Island." Newport, RI: C. E. Hammett Jr. 1852.

Ghosthunters, Season 9, episode 22. *Cumberland Library*.SyFy Network.

Ghosthunters, Season 8, episode 6. *Providence City Hall*.SyFy Network.

Grannon, Thomas. "Field of Dreams." National Trust of Historical Preservation, March 2004.

Green, Marcia. "Giants at Nine Men's Misery." *Valley Breeze*, November 19, 2014.

Haley, John Williams. *Old Stone Bank, History of Rhode Island vol. I.* Published by Institution for Savings. Prepared and Printed by Haley & Sykes Co. 1929

Haley, John Williams. *Old Stone Bank, History of Rhode Island vol. II.* Published by Institution for Savings. Prepared and Printed by Haley & Sykes Co. 1931

Harmon, Brigid. Archives Intern. "The Metropolitan Museum of Fine Arts Archives Durr Friedly Records 1906–1918."

Hart, Bertrand K. Columnist for *Providence Journal*, December 3, 1929.

Horsford, Eben Norton. *Defence of Norumbega*. Boston MA: Houghton, Mifflin, 1891.

Huget, Jennifer. "A Little Light Housekeeping." *Washington Post*, August 28, 2002.

Joshi, S. T., and David E. Schultz. *An H. P. Lovecraft Encyclopedia.* Westport CT: Greenwood Publishing Group, 2001.

Joshi, S. T., and Peter Cannon. *More Annotated H. P. Lovecraft. III Edition.* New York NY: Dell, 1999.

Krajicek, David J. "Rhode Island Rumrunner." *New York Daily News*, March 25, 2008.

Kelly, Jack. "Life and Death at Fort Adams." *Newport This Week*, August 29, 2013.

Lancaster, Jane. "Inquire Within: A Social History of the Providence Athenaeum Since 1753." Oak Knoll Press, 2003.

"The Lonely Ship." *Sunday Morning Star*, Wilmington DE, October 11, 1885.

McBurney, Christian. *Kidnapping the Enemy: The Special Operations to Capture General Charles Lee and Richard Prescott.* Yardley PA: Westholme Publishing, 2013.

McGinley, Morgan. "A New England Secret." *New York Times*, March 28, 1982.

The Merchants National Bank of Providence. "Old Providence, A Collection of Facts and Traditions Relating to Various Buildings and Sites of Historic Interest in Providence." Walton Advertising and Printing Company, Boston 1918.

Morrison, George Austin Jr. The New York Genealogical and Biographical Record, Vol. 38. New York Genealogical and Biographical Society, 1907.

"Must be a Doat." *Bristol Phoenix*, September 26, 1996.

Nayer, Melanie. "Get Spooked: Spend a Night in One of These Haunted Hotels." Boston.com, October 12, 2012.

Neslusan, Lauren. "The Dark Tunnels of Fort Wetherill." Examiner.com, March 24, 2010.

New England Journal of Medicine, Vol. 154.

New York Times. John Garland Obituary. September 4, 1906.

"Police on the Trail of Ghost." *Boston Evening Transcript*, July 18, 1906.

State of Rhode Island and Providence Plantation Preliminary Survey Report, Town of Portsmouth 1979.

Robinson, Charles Turek. *New England Ghost Files.* Covered Bridge Press, 1994.

Snyder, Paige. "13 Uniquely Rhode Island Superstitions." *East Side Monthly,* December 13, 2013.

Stedman, Thomas, Editor. "Medical Record, A Weekly Journal of Medicine and Surgery Vol. 69, January 6, 1906.

Tucker, Abigail. "The Great New England Vampire Panic." *Smithsonian Magazine,* October 2012.

Welty, Ellen. "Commune With the Unseen." *Rhode Island Monthly*, January 2015.

www.cliffwalk.com.

www.fortadams.org.

www.freemasonry.org.

www.geoffssuperlativesandwichesri.com.

www.hotelviking.com.

www.jamestownfd.com.

www.jamestownphilomenianlibrary.org.

www.leagle.com.

www.lighthousefriends.com.

www.narragansett.com.

www.newportgulls.com.

www.providenceathenaeum.org.

www.providenceartclub.org.

www.providencebiltmore.com.

www.prudencebayislandstransprt.com.

www.redwoodlibrary.org.

www.roseislandlighthouse.org.

www.seamensnewport.org.

www.swanpointcemetery.com.

www.thomastwerums.com.

www.trinitynewport.org.

www.whitehorsenewport.com.

Index